The Bliss of Inner Fire

THE BLISS OF INNER FIRE

Heart Practice of the Six Yogas of Naropa

LAMA THUBTEN YESHE

A Commentary on Je Tsongkhapa's

Having the Three Convictions: A Guide to the Stages
of the Profound Path of the Six Yogas of Naropa

FOREWORD BY LAMA ZOPA RINPOCHE
EDITED BY ROBINA COURTIN
AND AILSA CAMERON

Introduction by Jonathan Landaw

Wisdom

Wisdom Publications, Inc.
199 Elm Street
Somerville, Massachusetts 02144 USA
wisdomexperience.org

Library of Congress Cataloging-in-Publication Data
Thubten Yeshe, 1935–1984
  The bliss of inner fire : heart practice of the six yogas of
Naropa / by Lama Thubten Yeshe ; a commentary on Je Tsongkhapa's
Having the three convictions : a guide to the stages of the profound
path of the six yogas of Naropa.
    p. cm.
  Includes bibliographical references and index.
  ISBN 0–86171-136-x (alk. paper)
  1. Tso°-kha-pa Blo-bza°-grags-pa, 1357–1419. Zam lam N>-ro'i chos
drug gi sgo nas 'khrid pa'i rim pa yid ches gsum ldan ¤es bya ba.
2. N>˘ap>da. 3. Yoga (Tantric Buddhism) I. Tso°-kha-pa Blo-bza°-
grags-pa, 1357–1419. Zam lam N>-ro'i chos drug gi sgo nas 'khrid
pa'i rim pa yid ches gsum ldan ¤es bya ba.
BQ7950.N347T7838 1998
294.3'4436—dc21   98–6072

  ISBN 978-0-86171-136-9 ebook ISBN 978-0-86171-978-5

  23 22

  12 11 10

Cover design by Philip Pascuzzo.
Interior designed by Jennie Malcolm. Set in Diacritical Garamond 10.75/13.5.
Back cover photo: Lama Yeshe; photo ©Ricardo de Aratanha.

Wisdom Publications' books are printed on acid-free paper and meet the guidelines for permanence and durability of the Production Guidelines for Book Longevity of the Council on Library Resources.

Printed in the United States of America.

MIX
Paper from
responsible sources
FSC® C005010

Please visit fscus.org.

Contents

Foreword

By Lama Thubten Zopa Rinpoche

The unimaginable secret qualities and actions of a Buddha are the objects of knowledge only of the omniscient minds of other Buddhas. Therefore, there is no way that ordinary beings could understand Lama Yeshe's secret qualities; they could only see his qualities in accordance with the level of their mind. However, since individual experience is one of the most effective ways of realizing that the essence of the guru is Buddha, I would like to remember again the wonderful qualities of Lama Yeshe that I did have the karma to see.

❦ THE QUALITIES OF LAMA'S HOLY BODY

Even people who had never met Lama Yeshe got a very warm feeling simply from seeing a photograph of him; they immediately felt he was someone who was very kind and concerned about others. I once sent an English pen friend, Audrey Cohen, a photo of Lama in a group of monks. Although I didn't explain which of the monks was Lama, Audrey wrote to say that she got a good feeling from seeing a particular monk in the back row; this monk was Lama.

Many people reacted in a similar way to seeing Lama's holy body. Even though many Tibetans did not know who Lama Yeshe was and had not heard of his background as a great scholar, simply seeing Lama made them very happy, and they often felt devotion arise towards him. Once when we were visiting Bodhgaya some Tibetans from Sikkim met Lama in the street and immediately sensed a holy purity in him; they felt that he must be a great bodhisattva. The meeting had such a strong impact on them that they asked some nearby monks who Lama was, but no one really knew. That same evening one of the Tibetans came to see me and explained how impressed they had all been by meeting Lama in the street. He had incredible faith that Lama was a great holy being.

Simply seeing Lama's holy body brought peace and joy to the mind, and a wish to see more of him. Even without being introduced to him, people naturally respected Lama. Even people who had not met the Dharma felt that Lama was different from ordinary people. When they met Lama, they sensed very particular qualities of purity and holiness; they felt not only that he was learned but also that he had a deep spiritual quality.

In the general view, Lama's physical aspect changed with the development of his mind. For several years before he passed away, he looked very light and very radiant. This was an expression of his tantric realizations. Those who were aware of the signs could recognize the outer changes that were evidence of his inner development, especially of completion stage tantric realizations.

Even when Lama was showing the aspect of serious illness, he would suddenly look so bright and magnificent that you could almost think that he had no sickness at all. Out of his great compassion, Lama manifested various aspects as needed to subdue different sentient beings.

❧ THE QUALITIES OF LAMA'S HOLY SPEECH

Lama's holy speech was like nectar, and its power is the personal experience of those who received teachings from him. Every single word came out of his bodhicitta; every single word was for others.

When other Tibetan lamas give a public talk in the West, where there are usually people who are completely new to the Dharma, they often speak on subjects with which they are familiar rather than on subjects the people in the audience need to hear. Lama, however, would not usually talk on any one fixed subject but would address the various problems, spiritual and mundane, of the people in his audience.

Like offering a smorgasbord, Lama would speak on one subject, then switch to another, then another, without there necessarily being a connection between the subjects. Even though they might not like all the foods served, everybody would find something they liked among the various dishes. No matter what their social class or level of education, everybody received an answer to their problems that suited the nature of their mind. Even though they might have arrived with confused minds, they returned home extremely happy and satisfied. After an hour's talk from Lama, no one could walk away saying that they hadn't found the solution to their problems. This amazing skill is proof that Lama's holy action of teaching was Buddha's action.

It might appear to some people that Lama was simply telling many jokes to make people laugh, but those with a Dharma background appreciated how practical Lama's talks were. Someone who had been following Buddhadharma for twenty years and had heard many secret, profound teachings still found Lama's talks practical and beneficial. Lama's advice was not pie in the sky; it could be related to everyday life.

Some people came to Lama's lectures out of curiosity, just to see what a Tibetan lama looked like; they had no particular wish to receive teachings from a Tibetan lama or to study Buddha's teachings. Others came sincerely seeking peace of mind and some solution to the problems in their lives. From Lama's external appearance, they probably didn't expect him to have any methods to solve their problems. However, the more they listened to Lama, the more peaceful their minds became and the more they appreciated Lama's special qualities. Even someone with a mountain of pride in their own knowledge, which no one else could crush, would have their pride subdued by hearing Lama talk. They would naturally become more humble as a result of the teaching. At the same time, Lama himself had incredible humility, the quality of a learned person.

After Lama had talked for an hour, the people in the audience would realize that this Tibetan lama was remarkable, with extensive knowledge and many answers that they didn't have. During that hour they would be greatly inspired to learn more about Tibetan Buddhism; refuge in Dharma was actualized in their minds. Lama was unbelievably kind, because he planted the first inspiration to listen to the holy Dharma and then apply it in practice. From this inspiration comes enlightenment.

When Lama gave personal advice to his students, he would give each person exactly the advice they needed and make them extremely happy. Lama had an incredible ability to understand the various solutions that suited the level of mind of each person. When he advised people, Lama didn't rely upon dice and scriptures; his predictions came from his own wisdom.

When Lama taught introductory courses on lam-rim, the graduated path to enlightenment, the people listening to Lama talk felt that they could almost transform their minds into the realizations of the path to enlightenment. For example, when Lama gave teachings on bodhicitta even for a few minutes, because of his own realization of bodhicitta, the people in the audience felt as if they had achieved the realization of bodhicitta. It gave no freedom for the selfish attitude to arise.

It was similar when Lama taught on tantra. A sign of having attainments of the tantric path is that a practitioner's teachings on tantra are very clear and very effective. This was obvious when Lama taught on completion stage practices such as the Six Yogas of Naropa. Just by hearing Lama's teachings on the Six Yogas and doing one or two meditations, many students had experiences. The clarity and the effect of the teachings proved that they came out of Lama's experience of the tantric path.

This is the essence of the small understanding that an ordinary being could have of the qualities of Lama's holy speech. After listening to Lama speak, people felt no doubt that he was a holy being, a great bodhisattva. Just as the rising sun dispels the darkness from the earth, through his teachings Lama dispelled the darkness of ignorance from the minds of so many people.

❧ THE QUALITIES OF LAMA'S HOLY MIND

Lama had a very open heart and mind; he was open to all traditions of Tibetan Buddhism and to all religions. He had a very broad view and was also very farsighted. There was nothing tight, closed, or limited about Lama's approach to life. He was not someone walking a narrow road.

Even though Lama didn't have a reputation for being learned, he was respected by lamas from all orders of Tibetan Buddhism. Lama had an understanding of sutra and tantra not only according to the Gelug presentation but also according to the Nyingma, Sakya, and

Kagyu views. He was knowledgeable not only about Tibetan culture but also about Western culture and philosophy, which he had studied seriously. Lama was not confused by words and external appearances that seemed to imply differences between sutra and tantra and the various orders. He would check the meaning behind the words to reach his own understanding, then concentrate on putting that meaning into practice. This was a particular quality of Lama Yeshe.

The actual essence of Lama's holy mind was great compassion, just as it is with His Holiness the Dalai Lama. Lama was filled with great compassion, cherishing other sentient beings. You can understand Lama's great loving kindness from the way he took care of his students like babies. He was more than a mother, more than a father. Not only did he give teachings to his students, but he constantly encouraged them in their Dharma practice and helped them to solve their problems. Like a father, he would listen to all their problems and then give them personal advice as well as teachings. He wrote many letters each day, late at night, to give advice to students. Even though he had so many other things to do, Lama gave so much of his time and his life to solving the problems of his students and their families.

Lama would mix with people, entertaining them in whatever way made them happy and dissolving the tightness in their hearts. To make people happy he would go to the beach or to a restaurant. Because he did these things only to benefit others, they became causes for developing his own mind and realizations.

Lama told me that the whole point is to transform every action you do—eating, drinking, sleeping—into Dharma, so that your life becomes meaningful. Lama used to say that some beings even use their breathing to benefit others. Even though Lama didn't say so, I felt that he was actually describing his own qualities and experience, particularly his realization of bodhicitta.

Despite many doctors warning him of the seriousness of his heart condition, Lama was always extremely busy traveling, giving teachings, writing, reading texts, guiding the FPMT (Foundation for the Preservation of the Mahayana Tradition) Centers, and giving advice to students. When Lama was at Kopan Monastery, for example, even though he was concerned with giving guidance to all the Centers and to individual students, he would teach the Kopan monks; take care of their food and clothing; supervise what was happening in the kitchen and library; water the garden—and he still found time to wash the dogs with mange. He would accomplish so much in one day out of the unbearable compassion he felt for suffering sentient beings.

From the first time that Lama had x-rays in Kathmandu in the early 1970s, the doctors kept on telling him that he would not live long. The first doctor told Lama that his heart condition was so serious that he had only one year to live. Many other doctors later gave a similar diagnosis. However, even with this life-threatening physical condition, Lama lived for many years, during which he traveled extensively and engaged in many activities. Lama dedicated his life to others.

An ordinary person with such dangerously poor health could not have lived so long nor achieved so much. Because of the unbearable compassion he felt for his students, Lama tried to live as long as possible to guide his students and help them make their lives meaningful. While he was alive, he dedicated all his time and energy to others, day and night. Lama was able to live even when physically the situation seemed to be hopeless because of the power of his great bodhicitta, his strong will, and his tantric realizations.

Another of Lama's particular powers was the great scope of his vision; he had the ability to make huge plans to benefit the teachings and sentient beings. Many people could not comprehend the scale of these works and felt that the projects were too difficult to accomplish. When Lama's plans were actualized, however, they proved to be highly beneficial for those who had carried them out as well as for many other sentient beings. Such great works showed the qualities of Lama's holy mind: his great compassion, great will, capability, and understanding. If Lama had not had such a brave attitude to work for others, besides the planning and accomplishing of such projects, even the thought of them would not have arisen.

For me, one of Lama's most amazing qualities was that while he was so busy guiding all the FPMT Centers and individual students, his own practice and realizations did not degenerate. Month by month, year by year, Lama's practice actually developed. This incredible capability is one of the main causes of my faith in Lama. When

Lama visited each Center, he would see all the students and advise them, as well as take care of the Center itself. While working fully for others, doing hundreds of things, Lama would still be able to do his own practice, and there was always development of his realizations.

In some ways, it looks as if Lama was born with realizations of the three principal paths: renunciation, bodhicitta, and right view. Lama showed early signs of renunciation of this life. When he was a young child and had been in Sera Monastery for some time, he went back home to visit his family. Seeing the sufferings and hardships of family life and the big difference between being a monk and living a worldly lay life made him appreciate the incredible benefits of living in ordination. By visiting his family home, Lama developed renunciation and had not the slightest interest in worldly life.

Even though it looks as if Lama was born with bodhicitta, according to what he actually said, it seems he generated bodhicitta while receiving a *Lama Chöpa* commentary from His Holiness Trijang Rinpoche, the late Junior Tutor to His Holiness the Dalai Lama. Lama, along with the great meditator Gen Jampa Wangdu, Geshe Lama Könchog, and thousands of other monks, including many learned geshes and high lamas, received the *Lama Chöpa* commentary. After hearing this commentary, many geshes left the monastery and went to the nearby mountains to meditate and lead ascetic lives.

When it came to the commentary on the lam-rim prayer in *Lama Chöpa*, Lama said that he didn't find anything new in the section on impermanence and death. Nor did he find anything special in the part on renunciation. But when it came to the section on bodhicitta, equalizing and exchanging self for others, Lama said that he felt very strongly that this was the real teaching of Buddha, the very heart of Dharma.

Lama said that while he and Gen Jampa Wangdu were receiving these teachings, they did not waste their time; every day they meditated immediately after the sessions. In the general view, it looks as if Lama generated the realization of bodhicitta at that time.

When Gen Jampa Wangdu came to see Lama at Tushita Retreat Centre in Dharamsala, they often teased each other. Lama always put down ascetic monks, saying that even though they might physically be living on high mountains, their minds were clinging to worldly things. Lama would then say, "Oh, the whole world comes to me. I have everything and I enjoy it."

Gen Jampa Wangdu used to say, "Training the mind in the three principal paths is ancient talk." This meant that he had completed the realizations a long time ago. Lama would then reply, "Oh, I realized emptiness ages ago, when I was debating on Madhyamaka in the courtyard at Sera Je." Lama said that he realized emptiness when he was a young monk in Tibet.

In terms of tantric practice, Lama's main deity was Heruka Chakrasamvara. I didn't know very much about scriptures when Lama and I lived together at Buxa Duar,[1] but even at that time, when Lama was studying Buddha's rules of discipline, he was already reading many tantric texts. From the time that we came to Nepal from India in 1968, Lama read only tantric teachings, not so much on the generation stage of Heruka but on the completion stage. From time to time I would look at the texts he was reading. In 1975, on the second teaching tour to America, we stayed for a month in Madison, near Geshe Sopa Rinpoche's house, to have a holiday. During that time, Lama was reading various tantric texts dealing with the clear light. This indicates that Lama was experienced in these practices and had these attainments.

One of Lama's special qualities was that he never showed others that he was a great practitioner. Even to those close to him Lama did not show the external appearance of meditating. You never saw Lama sitting cross-legged in meditation posture for very long. He was either very active or relaxing. Lama, however, practiced very skillfully. Like Shantideva, he was a great hidden yogi. When Shantideva was at Nalanda, the other monks in the monastery thought that he spent his whole time doing only three things: eating, sleeping, and defecating. They did not think that Shantideva did any Dharma practice.

Like Shantideva, Lama kept his actual meditation hidden. Whether he was in the West or in the East, after lunch each day Lama would usually go to rest for one or two hours, but actually all those "naps" were meditation sessions. In the beginning I didn't realize what Lama was doing and thought his rest was just like ordinary sleep; then gradually I realized that it was actually meditation. The reality is that when Lama appeared to be sleeping at night and after lunch, he was practicing Dharma in a very skillful way.

I remember one day at Kopan when Yangtse Rinpoche's family came to visit us after lunch. Yangtse Rinpoche is the incarnation of a famous lama, Geshe Ngawang Gendun, who was one of Lama's teachers. Yangtse Rinpoche's father, Jampa Thinley, used to be in Lama's class in Tibet and was a close friend. Because of the visit, Lama didn't have time to rest after lunch, and after the family had left Lama said that he felt a great loss that he hadn't found time to rest. Lama appeared very sorry, like an ordinary person who had lost a big sack of gold. To someone who wasn't aware of Lama's hidden practice it looked as if Lama was clinging to the comfort of sleep. It didn't make sense to feel so sorry about having missed an hour of rest, especially for a Dharma practitioner.

Lama's "rest" had nothing to do with a physical problem or with karma and disturbing thoughts. It was to ensure the continuation of his realizations of the path. Once a practitioner has realizations, since the continuity of the experience needs to be maintained by meditating every day, even a few minutes of meditation becomes extremely precious.

The second last time that Lama was at Kopan, he went one day to rest in the small hut at the top of the hill. When he came back, Lama said, "It's strange. Normally I don't fall asleep, but this time I fell asleep for a few minutes and I dreamt that a powerful protector made offerings to me." This just slipped out, but it shows that when Lama rested after lunch he normally didn't go to sleep.

Also, Lama often said that it was important to eat foods such as curd, honey, garlic, and meat. I understood the reason for this only when I saw in Pabongka Dechen Nyingpo's *Collection of Notes* that meditators with realizations of the completion stage use these foods to develop the elements and drops in their body, so that they have stronger experiences of the clear light and strengthen the conditions for the illusory body. Lama ate these foods not to benefit his body but to develop his realizations. He was concerned not about external physical health but about inner mental health.

When Lama requested His Holiness Trijang Rinpoche for

teachings on the Six Yogas of Naropa, Rinpoche advised him to request the teachings from His Holiness the Dalai Lama, who had fresh experience of the practice. Lama received the teachings on the Six Yogas alone in His Holiness's private meditation room, which was a small, bare room. While receiving the teachings, Lama practiced and had many experiences.

Once in Dharamsala, when I had *lung*, or wind disease, Lama told me, "With achievement of bliss and voidness, there is no wind disease. There is no place for tightness if you have bliss in your heart." I think Lama was talking from his own experience. Great meditators, even when dealing with problems, experience no depression themselves because of their tantric realizations. I think Lama's realization of bliss and voidness overwhelmed the many problems he had to deal with in relation to the Dharma Centers and students. He was never depressed and was always very happy.

At the end of 1982, Lama taught the first course on the Six Yogas of Naropa at Istituto Lama Tzong Khapa in Italy. From that time, even though he didn't normally travel with *thangkas* and pictures, Lama always kept a particular picture of Lama Tsongkhapa with him. It was a common postcard, but Lama told me that it was very precious, and in my ordinary view he seemed to have much more devotion for Lama Tsongkhapa. When he returned from the course, Lama told me, "While I was at Istituto Lama Tzong Khapa, I did Heruka self-initiation every morning before I taught the Six Yogas of Naropa. It seemed to benefit the students very much. Because I read many scriptures, the teachings were very effective, and many people had experiences." During that time, Lama was reading the section on the illusory body from the completion stage of Guhyasamaja in Lama Tsongkhapa's *Lamp Thoroughly Illuminating the Five Stages*, which contains the most extensive teaching on the illusory body. Lama then added, "At this time I developed incredibly deep devotion for Lama Tsongkhapa because of his profound teachings."

Jacie Keeley, Lama's secretary, also told me that during the course at Istituto Lama Tzong Khapa, she noticed one morning that Lama was crying just as he was about to begin his teaching on the Six Yogas. After Lama returned from giving the teaching, Jacie asked him why he had been crying. Lama said, "I saw my guru." It seems that Lama saw His Holiness Trijang Rinpoche, his root guru, who had passed away more than a year before.

Lama wrote a poem in praise of Lama Tsongkhapa's clear explanations of the illusory body. Lama said that he had been unclear about how to achieve the illusory body until he had read Lama Tsongkhapa's writings on the subject. He felt that is was only by the kindness of Lama Tsongkhapa that the practices of the illusory body had been clarified. Lama also wrote a commentary on the Six Yogas of Naropa, but he did not complete it.

In my view, Lama achieved the illusory body when he was at Istituto Lama Tzong Khapa. I think so because Lama said that he had found incredible faith in Lama Tsongkhapa and because he then read texts solely on the illusory body, mostly from the Guhyasamaja Tantra. I relate Lama's devotion to Lama Tsongkhapa to the fact that Lama Tsongkhapa gave the clearest and most extensive explanations of how to achieve the illusory body.

When I looked through the texts that Lama took with him to Vajrapani Institute in mid-1983, when he taught the second course on the Six Yogas of Naropa, I found that they were all on Guhyasamaja and the illusory body. This indicates that Lama himself had achieved the illusory body.

Lama seemed to be able to read various texts in different rooms at the same time. When Lama was in retreat at Tushita Retreat Centre, for instance, he would have one text open in the retreat room, another open in the outer room, and yet another text open outside in the greenhouse. This reminded me of the stories His Holiness Zong Rinpoche told about meditators who had achieved the illusory body. While they were sleeping at night, they would use their subtle body to read and memorize many scriptures at the same time. I thought that Lama was able to read so many texts in such a short time because he did it at night with the illusory body. From the way Lama talked so confidently about the many actions that a yogi could do with their subtle body, I could see that Lama himself had this power.

When a new retreat house was being built at Tushita Retreat Centre, one morning a big fire suddenly started. The carpenters and other workers were trying to put the fire out with water, but everyone feared that it was burning out of control. At the time Lama was having breakfast nearby on the roof of his house with his brother, Geshe Thinley. Lama didn't even stand up to look at the fire. He just sat in his chair, quite relaxed. The rest of us were very worried, but Lama was not worried at all. When I went to Lama, he said, "The fire isn't a big danger. It won't cause any harm."

Even though the flames were very big, Lama remained relaxed, and he mentioned the story of a Tibetan monastery catching fire during Lama Tsongkhapa's time. Lama Tsongkhapa didn't need water or a lot of people to help him. He simply sat where he was and used his subtle body to put out the fire. I felt that the story was related to Lama's own actions to stop the danger from the fire.

Lama Yeshe was a great tantric practitioner, a real ascetic meditator, even though he didn't live alone in a cave. Lama was a great hidden yogi. He was a valid base to be labeled "yogi" not because he could perform tantric rituals but because he had unmistaken realizations of clear light and the illusory body. He reached the stage of tantra *mahamudra*.

Not long before he passed away, when Lama was considering whether to have a heart operation, he said, "It doesn't matter whether the operation is successful or not. I have used myself as a servant to others. I was able to do enough, and now I am completely satisfied. I have no worries."

This is a great teaching for us; it is the essential teaching of Lama Yeshe and of Guru Shakyamuni Buddha.

As Shantideva says in *A Guide to the Bodhisattva's Way of Life*:[2]

May I become a protector for those without one,
A guide for those who have entered the path;
May I become a bridge, a boat and a ship
For those who wish to cross over.

May I be an island for those who seek one
And a lamp for those needing light,

May I be a bed for all who wish to rest
And a servant for all who want a servant.

This was Lama's main teaching and exactly what he practiced all the time. This is Lama Yeshe's essential biography.

This foreword has been compiled from various talks given by Lama Thubten Zopa Rinpoche, the heart-disciple of Lama Yeshe.

Editors' Preface

The *Bliss of Inner Fire* combines the last two major teachings given by Lama Thubten Yeshe (1935–84), both commentaries on Lama Je Tsongkhapa's text *Having the Three Convictions,* itself a commentary on the Six Yogas of Naropa, a completion stage practice of Highest Yoga Tantra. Lama Yeshe's first teaching on the Six Yogas was given to 150 students at Istituto Lama Tzong Khapa, his center near Pomaia in Italy, during a three-week retreat-style course that began in mid-December 1982. In June 1983, Lama taught on the Six Yogas for two weeks to 100 students in another retreat-style course, this time at Vajrapani Institute, his center in northern California.

Lama Yeshe's main emphasis during both courses was on the practice of inner fire (Tib. *tummo*), the first of the Six Yogas. Lama said that covering all of the subjects in Lama Tsongkhapa's text was not his goal, and in fact he taught in detail only about a third of it. Before both courses, Lama gave a Heruka Chakrasamvara initiation, and he subsequently explained the inner fire techniques in relation to this deity.

During both courses, Lama gave an oral transmission of the text in Tibetan, interspersed with translations, experiential commentary, guided meditations, personal anecdotes, practical advice, jokes, pantomime, and much laughter. More than anything else, Lama wanted everybody to "taste" the practice of inner fire. He expected everybody to work hard and maintain a retreat regime. Between the discourses students meditated intensively on the techniques that had been explained, maintained periods of silence, and practiced the physical exercises associated with the practice. Again and again Lama stressed that he wanted everyone to act, to gain actual experience of inner fire, and not be content with mere intellectual understanding. He spent little time on the historical and philosophical background but was painstaking in his descriptions of the inner fire meditation techniques and the various preliminary practices.

Following the Introduction we have included a prayer traditionally used to invoke the blessings of the lineage lamas of the Six Yogas of Naropa.

In Part One, "The Six Yogas of Naropa," Lama inspires us to practice tantra, especially inner fire, the foundation stone of the entire tantric path. After giving brief but inspiring biographies of the mahasiddhas Naropa and Lama Tsongkhapa, Lama emphasizes the need to practice rather than intellectualize.

Part Two, "Preliminary Practices," deals briefly with the preliminaries to tantric practice: the common Mahayana preliminaries (the meditations of the graduated path to enlightenment) and the uncommon preliminaries (the general practices of receiving tantric initiation and observing vows and the specific tantric preliminaries of Vajrasattva practice and guru yoga).

Part Three, "Going Beyond Appearances," introduces the generation stage of Highest Yoga Tantra, which involves developing the divine pride and clear appearance of a meditational deity through training to transform the ordinary experiences of death, intermediate state, and rebirth into the pure experiences of a Buddha. In this section, Lama Yeshe also explains the characteristics of body and mind according to tantra, with special emphasis on understanding the absolute nature, or emptiness, of the mind.

Part Four, "Awakening the Vajra Body," discusses the actual preparatory practices for inner fire: the physical exercises that make the body serviceable; meditations on the channels, chakras, and syllables; and vase breathing meditation.

Part Five, "Discovering Totality," contains Lama's experiential teachings on the process of generating the inner fire; the culmination of the practice, the development of simultaneously born great blissful wisdom; and, with a brief discussion of the other five yogas, the completion of the tantric path to enlightenment.

Finally, in Part Six, "Living with Inner Fire," Lama Yeshe offers practical advice on how to bring the practice of inner fire into daily life.

We have chosen to accurately transliterate all mantras and syllables, and a Sanskrit pronunciation guide (p. 187) has been included to aid readers. However, the essential advice is to pronounce mantras in the same way as the lama who gives you the oral transmission of the mantra. For other Sanskrit words, we have used a spelling that approximates their pronunciation. Interested readers can consult the table of foreign word transliterations (p. 188) for the actual transliteration of these words.

We offer our heartfelt thanks to Lama Thubten Zopa Rinpoche, His Holiness Sakya Trizin, Kirti Tsenshab Rinpoche, Khen Jampa Tegchog, Geshe Lama Könchog, Khijo Rinpoche, Geshe Tashi Tsering, Geshe Norbu Dorje, and Khenpo Tsultrim Gyatso for their patience and kindness in clarifying various technical aspects of the practices.

We also thank His Holiness the Dalai Lama, the transcript of whose teaching on Lama Tsongkhapa's *Having the Three Convictions* in Dharamsala in 1990 was invaluable, as were Daniel Cozort's *Highest Yoga Tantra* and Glenn Mullin's *Tsongkhapa's Six Yogas of Naropa;* Glenn Mullin for his innumerable editorial suggestions; Ven. Sarah Thresher and Alfred Leyens for transcribing material contained in the foreword; Ven. Helmut Holm for transcribing the Istituto Lama Tzong Khapa teachings; Paula Chichester and Roger Munro for transcribing the Vajrapani Institute teachings; Karon Kehoe for her earlier editing of these teachings; David Molk, Geshe Lobsang Donyo, and Samten Chhosphel for their translation of the lineage lamas prayers and Khensur Lobsang Tharchin for his kind assistance in locating the text; Ven. George Churinoff, Ven. Thubten Samphel, Ven. Ngawang Jigdol, Ven. Connie Miller, Tubten Pende, Sonam Rigzin, Jon Landaw, Merry Colony, Robert Beer, Martin Brauen, and Jampa Gendun for their suggestions and help; Timothy McNeill and David Kittelstrom of Wisdom Publications; and Peter and Nicole Kedge, whose material support and encouragement helped us to realize the project.

May everyone who reads *The Bliss of Inner Fire* be inspired to seek a tantric master, enter the supreme tantric path, and quickly achieve enlightenment for the sake of all living beings. As Lama said at the very end of the Vajrapani Institute course, nine months before he passed away, "If I am alive and you are alive, perhaps we will see each other again. The next time we will discuss in detail the illusory body, the dream experience, the clear light experience, transference of consciousness, and consciousness going into another body. These subjects are more profound and sophisticated. You should work now on what we have already covered, and we will pray that at some time we will do the rest of the Six Yogas of Naropa. If we cannot do them next year, we can do them next life."

Introduction

by Jonathan Landaw

I n 1987 Wisdom Publications brought out a volume by Lama Thubten Yeshe entitled *Introduction to Tantra*. In that work, a compilation of excerpts from numerous teachings given by Lama Yeshe between 1975 and 1983, the reader was offered a glimpse into the profound, and often misunderstood, world of Tibetan Tantric Buddhism. With clear and inspiring discussions of such topics as the basic purity of the mind, the means for recognizing and overcoming our limiting thought patterns, the self-transformational techniques of tantric deity-yoga meditation and so forth, Lama Yeshe presented the tantric vision of totality in a form accessible to as wide an audience as possible. In that introductory work it was his intention to convey the flavor of these most advanced Buddhist teachings in such a way that spiritual seekers, regardless of their cultural background or religious affiliation, might be motivated to discover their own basic purity, fulfill their highest potential, and be of maximum benefit to others.

Included in *Introduction to Tantra* were a number of passages selected from the last two major teachings given by Lama Yeshe before his passing. These teachings had been delivered at Istituto Lama Tzong Khapa in Pomaia, Italy, in 1982 and at Vajrapani Institute in Boulder Creek, California, in 1983. Their focus was the inner fire practices of Highest Yoga Tantra—the fourth and most advanced level of tantra—as set forth in the famed Six Yogas of Naropa and elucidated in Je Tsongkhapa's commentary on the Six Yogas entitled *Having the Three Convictions*. The current work, *The Bliss of Inner Fire*, is an amalgamation of these two final teachings.

❦ SOURCE OF THE TEACHINGS

Although the practices of inner fire explained in this work can be traced back to the Six Yogas of the famed eleventh-century Buddhist scholar and tantric adept, Pandit Naropa, after which they are named, we should not think that they were his creation. Instead, as is the case with all authentic teachings of Buddhist tantra, they ultimately derive from Shakyamuni Buddha himself, the so-called historical Buddha who lived 2,500 years ago (563–483 B.C.E.). However, as His Holiness the Fourteenth Dalai Lama has stated in *The World of Tibetan Buddhism,*

> We need not presume that all of the teachings of tantra were propounded by the Buddha during his historical lifetime. Rather, I think that the teachings of tantra could have also emerged through the extraordinary insights of highly realized individuals who were able to explore to the fullest extent the physical elements and the potential within the human body and mind. As a result of such investigation, a practitioner can attain very high realizations and visions, thus enabling him or her to receive tantric teachings at a mystical level. Therefore, when we reflect on tantric teachings, we should not limit our perspective by rigid notions of time and space. (p. 93)

Both Naropa—the Indian mahasiddha, or greatly accomplished one—and the Tibetan master Je Tsongkhapa (1357–1419) are numbered among the "highly realized individuals" referred to by the Dalai Lama and were, therefore, capable of receiving instructions on such profound practices as inner fire directly from the enlightened source.

The principal form that Shakyamuni Buddha assumes when presenting the advanced teachings of tantra is that of Vajradhara—the Holder of the Diamond Scepter—who is sometimes called the Buddha of the Tantras. In general, the blessings, instructions, and realizations of these tantric teachings come down to the present via two types of lineage: the distant and the close. The former is comprised of the successive guru-disciple relationships that link one generation with the next, the realized disciple of a particular master becoming mentor to disciples of his or her own. In terms of the tantric teachings we are concerned with here, this generation-to-generation lineage, beginning with Buddha Vajradhara, includes such famous Indian mahasiddhas as Saraha, Nagarjuna, Ghantapa, and Tilopa.

As for the so-called close lineages, these come about in the more immediate manner indicated previously. In Naropa's case, he not only received tantric initiation, or empowerment, from his human guru, Tilopa, but was able to establish communication with Buddha Vajradhara directly; the Buddha of the Tantras manifested to him in the form of such tantric meditational deities as Hevajra, Heruka Chakrasamvara, and Vajrayogini. As for Je Tsongkhapa, he was not only heir to the lineage of Indian, Nepalese, and Tibetan masters that spanned the four hundred years separating him from Naropa, but he also received inspiration from Vajradhara through his own patron deity, Manjushri, the embodiment of the wisdom of all enlightened beings. Thus the teachings we know as the Six Yogas of Naropa, including the inner fire practices that are the main subject matter of this present work, should not be considered the later fabrications of Indian gurus or Tibetan lamas but are ultimately rooted in the enlightened realizations of Shakyamuni Buddha himself, passed down in unbroken lineages of realized practitioners to the present day.

❦ THE AUTHOR AND HIS STYLE OF TEACHING

Lama Thubten Yeshe began his Buddhist training at Sera Monastery, one of the three great institutions of learning and practice founded by Je Tsongkhapa and his disciples in the vicinity of Lhasa, the capital of Tibet. After the Chinese takeover of Tibet in the 1950s, he completed his formal training at the Buxa Duar refugee camp in northeastern India. Unlike most of his fellow monks at Sera, who confined their studies to the Gelug tradition founded by Je Tsongkhapa, Lama Yeshe was greatly interested in teachings by masters of all traditions. His open-minded, nonsectarian approach is attested to by the fact that while at Buxa Duar his own students included lamas from these various traditions.

The Buddhist education Lama Yeshe received had two major

divisions. The first of these is called sutra and is named after those teachings, or discourses—such as the *Prajñāpāramitā Sutras*, or *Discourses on the Perfection of Wisdom*—in which Shakyamuni Buddha set forth the various aspects of the general path leading to full spiritual awakening. The course of study at the Tibetan monasteries included not only these teachings by Buddha himself but the commentaries on them by such Indian masters as Chandrakirti (*Guide to the Middle Way*), Maitreya/Asanga (*Ornament of Clear Realizations*), Shantideva (*A Guide to the Bodhisattva's Way of Life*), Atisha (*Lamp on the Path to Enlightenment*) and many others. Through study, debate, and meditation upon these texts and the later commentaries on them by a succession of Tibetan masters, and through intimate exposure to the authentic oral traditions enlivening these texts, students at Sera and the other monasteries had the opportunity of gaining insight into and realization of the vast and profound meaning of Buddha's teachings.

With the foundation in moral discipline, logical analysis, compassionate motivation, insightful wisdom, and so forth provided by these sutra studies, well-qualified practitioners were able to delve into the second of the two major divisions of their education: the profound study of tantra. The Sanskrit term "tantra" is applied to those advanced teachings of Buddha Shakyamuni/Vajradhara by means of which the full enlightenment of Buddhahood, the ultimate goal of all Buddhist paths, can be attained in the shortest time possible. Each tantra focuses upon a meditational deity embodying a particular aspect of enlightened consciousness; in Lama Yeshe's case, he received empowerment and instructions in such tantras as those of the meditational deities Heruka Chakrasamvara, Vajrayogini, Vajrabhairava, and Guhyasamaja and studied the famous Six Yogas of Naropa following *Having the Three Convictions*, a commentary based on the personal experiences of Je Tsongkhapa, as cited above. He received the lineage blessings of these practices from some of the greatest tantric masters of the day, including Kyabje Ling Dorjechang (1903–83) and Kyabje Trijang Dorjechang (1901–81), the Senior and Junior Tutors, respectively, of His Holiness the Fourteenth Dalai Lama (b. 1935).

Lama Yeshe did not merely study these profound tantric teachings, he put them into practice in extensive meditational retreats and in his daily life. As became clear to many toward the end of his life, his main practice was that of Heruka Chakrasamvara, and he devoted much time and energy to gaining deeper and deeper realizations of this Highest Yoga Tantra. According to his heart-son and disciple, Lama Thubten Zopa Rinpoche, Lama Yeshe wrote privately about his own meditational experiences of both Heruka Chakrasamvara and the Six Yogas of Naropa and would often speak to Lama Zopa about clear light and bliss, the essence of these advanced tantric practices.

It is not surprising, then, that the last two major teachings Lama Yeshe gave were on the inner fire practices of the Six Yogas, through which the blissful experience of the clear light is attained, and that he opened each of these teachings with an empowerment into the tantra of Heruka Chakrasamvara. Nor is it surprising that the final practice he himself engaged in, up until his heart stopped beating, was that of Heruka Chakrasamvara. What is particularly inspiring, however, is that through his mastery of the blissful clear light consciousness dawning at the time of death, Lama Yeshe was able to pass away and be reborn in a state of full conscious control, even to the point of choosing as his future parents two students of his who had helped establish a meditation center in Spain called Osel Ling, the Place of Clear Light. Their son, Tenzin Osel Rinpoche, born in 1985, was recognized as the reincarnation of Lama Yeshe by His Holiness the Dalai Lama.

Although the practices of inner fire belong to the most advanced branch of the Buddhist teachings, Lama Yeshe often presented them, in simplified form, even to his newest students. He did this to give them a taste of the inexhaustible treasure of blissful energy existing within each and every one of us right at the present moment. Although such blissful energy, by itself, cannot liberate us from the vicious circle of dissatisfaction and suffering, our ability to experience it directly—to "taste the chocolate," as he would often say—can have a significant and beneficial effect upon us. Such an experience convinces us, as no merely philosophical investigation can, of the profound changes we can bring about simply by gaining control over our mind in meditative concentration. The inspiration provided by such direct experience can empower our entire spiritual practice.

The courses in Italy and California, from which the material in this book has been taken, were run as meditational retreats, and Lama Yeshe's lectures were designed to guide and encourage the participants in their efforts to gain an actual experience, rather than a mere intellectual understanding, of what meditation has to offer. The emphasis was on clarifying the instructions of the Six Yogas, without an in-depth examination of their historical significance or philosophical basis. Because most of the course participants were already familiar with the necessary preparatory material through previous exposure to Buddhist teachings, the way was clear to focus single-pointedly on the step-by-step practices of inner fire itself. So, in a sense, *The Bliss of Inner Fire* is like a second *Introduction to Tantra*, opening up the world of Highest Yoga Tantra's advanced practices the way the earlier work opened up the world of tantra in general.

The present work, in addition to dealing with more advanced subject matter, differs from its predecessor in that it concentrates on specific technical aspects of tantric practice. As the reader will discover, *The Bliss of Inner Fire* offers detailed instructions on the various phases of inner fire meditation. This emphasis on meditational instruction makes the present work a valuable manual for those interested in engaging in serious and prolonged practice themselves. However, because many readers will lack the background necessary for a full appreciation of these teachings, it may be helpful to introduce Lama Yeshe's instructions with a few remarks about the tantric path in general and the place within this path of the yoga of inner fire.

✼ AN OVERVIEW OF THE PATH

To begin with, the ultimate purpose of all Buddhist teachings is to lead others to enlightenment, or Buddhahood. This fully purified and expansive state of consciousness is characterized by limitless compassion, wisdom, and skillful means; the Mahayana, or Great

Vehicle, teachings of Shakyamuni Buddha stress that only by attaining such complete awakening of mind and heart can we fulfill our own innate spiritual potential and, more important, be of maximum benefit to others.

As already stated, the Mahayana presents two interrelated approaches to this full and complete enlightenment: the more general path of sutra and the esoteric path of tantra. The sutra vehicle (Skt. *Sutrayana*) sets forth methods whereby the obscurations veiling one's innate purity of mind are gradually removed, like peeling away the layers of an onion. At the same time, the mind's positive qualities of love, compassion, wisdom, and so forth are gradually enhanced so that eventually one attains a state beyond the limitations of ordinary, egocentric consciousness.

The trainings in nonattachment, compassionate altruism, and penetrative insight so vital to Sutrayana practice form the foundation of the tantric vehicle as well. But Tantrayana—also known as Mantrayana and Vajrayana—is distinguished from Sutrayana by being a so-called resultant vehicle. That is to say, the qualified practitioner of tantra is empowered to take the future result of the path, the experience of enlightenment itself, as the very basis of his or her practice. In place of the ordinary, limited self-image, the tantric trainee cultivates the powerful vision of having already attained full enlightenment in the form of a particular meditational deity (Tib. *yidam*). All the elements of ordinary experience—one's surroundings, sensory enjoyments, and activities—are likewise viewed as having undergone a similar enlightened transformation. Everything is seen as pure and blissful, just as a Buddha would experience it. By training in this way it is possible to achieve the actual result of full enlightenment much more swiftly than by relying on the Sutrayana approach alone.

The theme of enlightened transformation pervades the vast scope of tantric teachings and practices. Energies and states of mind that are considered negative and antithetical to spiritual growth according to other religious paths are transformed by the alchemy of tantra into forces aiding one's inner development. Chief among these is the energy of desire. According to the fundamental teachings of

Sutrayana, desirous attachment only serves to perpetuate the sufferings of samsara: the vicious circle of uncontrolled life and death, born from ignorance and fraught with dissatisfaction, within which unenlightened beings trap themselves. Therefore, if one truly wishes to be free from this samsaric cycle of misery, it is necessary to eliminate the poison of desirous attachment from one's heart and mind completely. While the Tantrayana agrees that ultimately all such ignorantly generated desires must be overcome if freedom and enlightenment are to be achieved, it recognizes the tremendous energy underlying this desire as an indispensable resource that can, with skill and training, be utilized so that it empowers rather than interferes with one's spiritual development.

Of course, any path utilizing the powerful and potentially destructive energies of desire and the other delusions is dangerous indeed. If followed improperly or with a selfish motivation, tantra can lead the misguided practitioner into realms of mental and physical suffering of unimaginable enormity. That is why even though tantric techniques may be outlined in a book such as this, they can only be followed safely and productively under the watchful eye of a fully qualified tantric master, and only by those who cultivate a particularly powerful altruistic motivation, receive the requisite empowerments, keep purely their tantric pledges, and undergo the proper preliminary trainings. It is said that for those who do rely on an accomplished tantric master and observe the precepts of tantric practice purely, it is possible to reach the goal of full enlightenment within the space of one short human lifetime, even within a few years.

Not all the tantric systems have equal power in propelling their trainees along the path to enlightenment. Instead, tantra is divided into four progressive classes—(1) Action, (2) Performance, (3) Yoga, and (4) Highest Yoga—and it is only through the pure practice of a system belonging to the supreme class of Highest Yoga Tantra that full enlightenment can be attained in the swiftest possible manner. What chiefly differentiates these four classes from one another is the varying abilities of their respective trainees to utilize desire on the spiritual path. While followers of the lower classes of tantra can control and utilize only the less passionate levels of attachment—

traditionally likened to the desire aroused when (1) looking at, (2) laughing with, and (3) embracing an attractive partner—the qualified practitioner of Highest Yoga Tantra is one who can channel into the path of spiritual evolution energies as intense as those associated with (4) sexual union itself.

Harnessing desire in Highest Yoga Tantra is accomplished in two successive levels of practice: the evolutionary stage and the completion stage. The former, also known as the generation stage, serves as a preparation and rehearsal for the latter and involves, among other things, cultivating what are known as the clear appearance and divine pride of one's chosen meditational deity. For example, if one is following the tantra of the wrathful male deity Heruka Chakrasamvara, one practices overcoming the ordinary view of oneself as a limited, samsaric being and cultivates in its place the enlightened self-image of actually being this powerful deity. This not only involves gaining familiarity with the various qualities of Chakrasamvara's body, speech, and mind so that one can experience oneself as possessing these attributes, but also demands a degree of mastery in meditation upon ultimate truth: *shunyata*, or emptiness.

The subject of emptiness is too vast to go into in any great deal here. Suffice it to say for now that it involves ridding the mind of all falsely conceived, fantasized modes of existence arising from ignorance of the way in which things actually do exist. It is fundamental to all Buddhist systems of practice, whether sutra or tantra, to recognize that the limited, concrete view we have of ourselves and our surroundings is in the nature of ignorance and therefore the source of all suffering; all such misconceptions must be overcome if we are ever to achieve lasting liberation from samsaric dissatisfaction. As Lama Yeshe declared in *Introduction to Tantra*, "As long as we are burdened by these misconceptions, we remain trapped in the world of our own projections, condemned to wander forever in the circle of dissatisfaction we have created for ourselves. But if we can uproot these wrong views and banish them completely, we will experience the freedom, space and effortless happiness we presently deny ourselves" (p. 69).

As stated, then, the practice of tantra involves a combination of emptiness-yoga—through which all ordinary conceptions of oneself are dissolved—and deity-yoga—in which one cultivates the enlightened identity of a particular meditational deity. As the Dalai Lama points out in *The World of Tibetan Buddhism*, "A unique characteristic of…Highest Yoga Tantra is that it employs in its profound path various meditative techniques that have corresponding similitudes not only to the resultant state of Buddhahood, that is, to the three kayas, but especially to the bases of purification on the ordinary level of human existence—for example, death, intermediate state, and rebirth" (p. 125).

These correspondences are outlined in the accompanying table and the significance of the three Buddha bodies (*kaya*) can be explained briefly as follows. The attainment of full enlightenment, or Buddhahood, is said to accomplish two purposes: those of oneself and those of others. With enlightenment comes the elimination of all obscurations of the mind, which are created by ignorance and produce suffering, as well as the enhancement of limitless beneficial qualities such as blissful awareness and universal compassion; this perfection of consciousness completely fulfills the practitioner's own purpose for following the spiritual path. But such an extremely subtle, unobstructed, and fully evolved consciousness—the truth body, or *dharmakaya*, of a Buddha—can fulfill the needs of others only if it manifests in forms to which those not yet fully enlightened can relate. Therefore, with the compassionate motive to benefit others, there first emerges from the unobstructed sphere of dharmakaya the subtle enjoyment body (*sambhogakaya*), which only higher bodhisattvas can perceive, and then the grosser emanation body (*nirmanakaya*), which even ordinary beings can contact. It is through the guidance and inspiration provided by these two form bodies (*rupakaya*) that the purposes of others are accomplished.

The three times	Meditative vision	Buddha body
Death/sleep	Clear light	Wisdom body
Intermediate state/ dream	Seed-syllable or shaft of light	Enjoyment body
Rebirth/reawakening	Meditational deity	Emanation body

During the evolutionary stage of Highest Yoga Tantra, the practitioner simulates the movement from death, through the intermediate state (Tib. *bardo*), to rebirth—which also corresponds to the movement from sleep, through dreams, to reawakening—in such a way that these three times are taken into the path and regarded as the three bodies of a Buddha. Although one contemplates deeply upon the increasingly subtle states of consciousness experienced during death and upon the transformations associated with the intermediate state and rebirth, these changes do not actually occur at this time. Instead, these evolutionary stage practices serve as a rehearsal for the actual transformations that take place only during the advanced levels of the completion stage. For it is during the completion stage that one gains control over the elements of the vajra body—the subtle channels, winds, and drops existing within the envelope of the gross physical body—and with this control comes the ability not merely to simulate the death experience but to bring about the actual transformations of consciousness occurring during that experience.

All completion stage practices are directly or indirectly associated with the meditative technique known as inner fire, the main subject matter of this present volume. Through mastery of inner fire, one can gain full conscious control over the vajra body and the ability to bring the mind to its most subtle and penetrating state: the blissful clear light experience. This extraordinarily powerful state of mind is unequaled in its ability to gain direct, penetrative insight into ultimate truth and thereby eliminate all afflictive states of mind.

Through the profound completion stage practices, the activities of one's body, speech, and mind become the natural resources of unprecedented spiritual growth as all forms of desirous energy are channeled into the path. Eventually one develops the ability to negotiate the hazards of death and beyond with complete awareness and control. And finally, at the culmination of the path, one attains the blissful state of unlimited awareness known as full enlightenment, spontaneously and effortlessly fulfilling one's compassionate intention to work for the welfare of all other beings. In this way the promise of one's inner potential for limitless compassion, wisdom, and skill is realized and one's life becomes truly meaningful.

This extremely brief summary of some of the major points of tantric practice should provide a context within which the following explanations of the inner fire teachings of the Six Yogas of Naropa can be more fully appreciated. For a more detailed discussion of these points, the reader is referred to the list of selected additional reading at the end of this text (p. 221). And those whose interest has been sufficiently whetted can do nothing better then search out reliable tantric masters for themselves and receive from them personal instruction in the entire range of sutra and tantra practices.

Prayer
to the Lineage Lamas of the Six Yogas of Naropa

Glorious and precious root lama,
Please sit on the lotus of my heart
And caring for me with your great kindness,
Bestow attainments of body, speech, and mind.

Heruka, pervasive lord of the mandala of great bliss,
Tilopa, who fully realized bliss and emptiness,
And Naropa, embodiment of Heruka himself,
I implore you to bestow upon me the wisdom of bliss and emptiness.

Marpa, crown jewel of vajra holders,
Milarepa, who attained the vajra state,
And Gampopa, supreme within the vajra family,
I implore you to bestow upon me the wisdom of bliss and emptiness.

Pagmo Drupa, great lord of living beings,
Jigten Sumgön, guide of living beings,
Rechungpa, who accomplishes the welfare of living beings,
I implore you to bestow upon me the wisdom of bliss and emptiness.

Jampa Pel, lord of translators,
Sönam Wangpo, treasury of the Dharma's meaning,
Sönam Senge, expounder of language and logic,
I implore you to bestow upon me the wisdom of bliss and emptiness.

Yang Tsewa, who beheld the meaning of the scriptures,
Butön Rinchen Drup, crown jewel of sages,
Jampa Pel, great sage and siddha,
I implore you to bestow upon me the wisdom of bliss and emptiness.

Dragpa Wangchug, endowed with the eye of Dharma,
Omniscient Losang Dragpa, King of Dharma,
Great Khedrub Je, the supreme Dharma son,
I implore you to bestow upon me the wisdom of bliss and emptiness.

Venerable Baso Chögyen, who has perfect intelligence,
Chökyi Dorje, who found total liberation,
Losang Döndrup, the great guide of all,
I implore you to bestow upon me the wisdom of bliss and emptiness.

Sangye Yeshe, who destroys misconceptions,
All seeing Losang Chökyi Gyeltsen,
Damchö Gyeltsen, who has abandoned all delusion,
I implore you to bestow upon me the wisdom of bliss and emptiness.

Wangchug Menkangpa, the secret yogi,
Nada, who manifests the great secret path,
Ngawang Jampa, holder of the treasury of secrets,
I implore you to bestow upon me the wisdom of bliss and emptiness.

Yeshe Gyeltsen, the holy tutor,
Ngawang Tenpa, master of Buddha's entire teachings,
Yeshe Tenzin, guide to all of tantra,
I implore you to bestow upon me the wisdom of bliss and emptiness.

Manjushila, manifestation of all Buddhas,
Maitri, who makes Buddha's profound teachings flourish,
Kelsang Tenzin, the great son of Buddha,
I implore you to bestow upon me the wisdom of bliss and emptiness.

Having well realized that tantra's meaning is inseparable method
    and wisdom,
And trained the mind with method, the profound vital points of
    the path,
Skillful guide of living beings, Chökyi Dorje,
I implore you to bestow upon me the wisdom of bliss and emptiness.

By single-pointedly practicing in no one place,
You became a supreme lord of siddhas who fully experiences the
    definitive meaning.
Revealer of the path to the definitive secret, Padma Dorje,
I implore you to bestow upon me the wisdom of bliss and emptiness.

You embody the gross and subtle channels, the dakas and dakinis,
All root and lineage lamas, as well as the Three Jewels,
O root lama Dechen Nyingpo,
I implore you to bestow upon me the wisdom of bliss and emptiness.

Chakrasamvara, all pervasive lord of great bliss,
Supreme Vajravarahi, bestower of the four blisses,
Dakas and dakinis who always enjoy great bliss,
I implore you to bestow upon me the wisdom of bliss and emptiness.

Life is impermanent, like lightning in the sky,
And all good things gained in samsara must be left behind.
Seeing this, bless me that my mind turns toward Dharma,
And, exasperated, I develop the determination to be free.

My poor old mothers are exhausted by mental and physical pain
Experienced for my sake over countless lifetimes.
Bless me to develop the compassionate wish to free them and
    bodhicitta,
And to transcend through the ways of a bodhisattva.

Bless me to develop constant and effortless admiration
And devotion for the kind lama, root of all attainments,
And to protect whatever vows and commitments
I have received as I dearly protect my life.

With whatever appears manifesting as the mandala of the deity,
Bless my mind to be ripened
Through actualizing the experience of great bliss
And realizing the nature of all things, free from elaboration.

By drawing the fresh winds through outer and inner methods
Into the central channel and igniting the wild one's fire,
Bless me to realize the simultaneously born bliss
That arises from contact with the melting kundalini.

Bless me so that the sleep in which my gross mind and breath
      have ceased
Becomes the nature of the clear light of bliss and emptiness,
And that everything wished for arises without obstruction,
Such as illusory body emanation in bardo-like dreams.

Having attained the glorious bliss of simultaneously born clear light,
With the clear drop arising as the venerable deity and consort,
Having manifest the miraculous web,
Bless me to attain unification in this life.

If death occurs through force of karma,
Bless me to generate confidence to recognize the mother and child
      clear lights,
And, arising in the bardo as the sambhogakaya,
Through miraculous emanations may I guide living beings.

Bless me to accomplish the concentration of transference of
      consciousness,
From the path of Brahma, into space, to the pure land of the dakinis,
And to accomplish the yoga of entering
The abode of another's aggregates, just as I choose.

Cared for with compassion by Glorious Heruka and consort
As well as the dakinis of the three places,
May all outer and inner obstacles be pacified, conducive conditions
      established,
And may I swiftly complete the two stages of the excellent path.

May all be auspicious!

❧ THE ABBREVIATED LINEAGE PRAYER

Great Vajradhara, Tilopa, Naropa,
Marpa, Milarepa, and Dharma Master Gampopa,
Pagmo Drupa, the Victor Drikungpa.
Supplication to the direct and lineage lamas.

You embody the gross and subtle channels, the dakas and dakinis,
All root and lineage lamas, as well as the Three Jewels,
O root lama Dechen Nyingpo,
I implore you to bestow upon me the wisdom of bliss and
    emptiness.

In this very life, bless me to actualize
All the realizations of the glorious Six Yogas of Naropa,
These supreme instructions, combining hundreds of thousands
Of streams of the profound essential nectar of the father and
    mother tantras.

PART ONE

The Six Yogas of Naropa

1. Tantra and Inner Fire

Lord Buddha taught the path to enlightenment at many different levels, in accordance with the variety of needs and capabilities of sentient beings. To give his most advanced teachings, known as Tantrayana or Vajrayana, he manifested in his esoteric aspect of Vajradhara. Tantrayana is the quickest vehicle to full enlightenment.

According to Lord Buddha's general teachings, known as Sutrayana, desire is the cause of human beings' problems, so it must be avoided. According to Tantrayana, however, this very desire can be used in the path to enlightenment. On the basis of strong renunciation, the great compassion of bodhicitta, and the right view of emptiness, tantric practitioners use the energy of their own pleasure as a resource and, in the deep concentration of *samadhi* meditation, unify it with the wisdom that realizes emptiness. Eventually this gives rise to simultaneously born great blissful wisdom, which in turn leads to enlightenment.

In tantra we are dealing with pleasure, not with pain. The person who is qualified to practice tantra is able to cope with pleasure, to experience pleasure without losing control, to utilize it. This is the essential characteristic of the tantric personality. Tantra does not work for people who are miserable, because they have no resource of pleasure to utilize.

In tantric practice, we work with the energy of our own human body. This resource is composed of six factors: the four elements (earth, water, fire, and air), the channels of our subtle nervous system, and the blissful *kundalini* drops that exist within the channels.[1] The human body is the gold mine of tantra; it is our most precious possession.

What we need is a skillful method to harness this powerful energy so that we can achieve not only more and more satisfaction in our everyday lives, but eventually the total satisfaction of full enlightenment. What we need is the practice of inner fire.

Inner fire is the first subject in the set of tantric practices known as the Six Yogas of Naropa. The other five are the yogas of the illusory body; clear light; transference of consciousness; transference into another body; and the intermediate state, or bardo. During this teaching, my main emphasis will be on the yoga of inner fire.

In Tibetan we say that inner fire is *lam kyi mang-do,* "the foundation stone of the path." It is fundamental to the realizations of the illusory body and clear light—to the realizations, in fact, of all the advanced completion stage practices of tantra. I will discuss this in more detail later; but, in short, in order to achieve enlightenment we use the practice of inner fire to cause all the airs, or vital energies, within our body to enter, stabilize, and absorb in the central channel of our subtle nervous system. This leads to the experience of simultaneously born great bliss. This bliss—which is not mere sentimental pleasure but a profound experience beyond our ordinary imagination—is then unified with the wisdom that understands emptiness in a process that eventually leads to the union of the illusory body and the absolute clear-light wisdom, and finally to full enlightenment.

Inner fire is *tummo* in Tibetan, and the literal meaning of tummo is "brave female." *Tum* means courage or bravery; *mo,* used in Tibetan grammar as a female modifier, represents the wisdom of nonduality. Tummo is courageous because it destroys all delusions and superstitions and female because it enables our subtlest level of consciousness to realize simultaneously born great blissful wisdom. This is the essential purpose of tantric practice, and inner fire can help us to achieve it.

Inner fire meditation really suits the Western mind because Westerners like to work with material, with energy. You like to play with it, fix it, change it, manipulate it. With inner fire you are doing exactly that; but the difference is that you are playing with your inner energy, your own pleasure resource.

Also, Westerners like instant satisfaction. It's what you expect. Well, inner fire gives you this. It is the direct path to enlightenment that you have heard about. It is a very simple process: very practical, very scientific, and very logical. You don't have to believe that inner fire brings bliss for it to work; you just do the practice and get the results.

The lam-rim, the step-by-step presentation of the path to enlightenment, brings satisfaction in a more religious way; inner fire is more scientific because actualizing it does not depend upon religious belief. If you act, the experience automatically comes. No customs or rituals are involved. With inner fire, you are dealing directly with your own inner reality; you are simply increasing the power of the kundalini and heat energy that you already possess. It is amazingly powerful, like a volcano erupting from within you.

The philosophy and methods of lam-rim are presented intellectually, and to some extent you can be intellectually convinced. But this conviction is like a cloud in the sky. When it is there, your spiritual practice is strong; but when the cloud disappears, you get discouraged, and your practice becomes weak. After being oriented towards lam-rim, when you hear that inner fire meditation is the fundamental path leading to the realization of enlightenment, you are suddenly in a new world.

Inner fire is the real chocolate! Whereas you may find it difficult to get results with other meditations, inner fire is a sensitive, quick way to convince yourself that you are progressing. It will surprise you. When you practice it you will think, "What else do I need? This is the only way." Other practices will seem second-rate. Sutrayana explains detailed meditation techniques for developing deep samadhi, but it has nothing to compare to inner fire meditation, which brings an explosion of nonduality wisdom, an explosion of bliss. Concentrating on a sensation or even on the Buddha is fine, but it can't lead you to the greatest realization of simultaneously born great blissful wisdom.

Inner fire is like the main door leading into a complex of hundreds of treasure houses. All the facilities for magnetizing realizations are there. Since it penetrates the very center of the universe of the body, it is incredibly sensitive in producing realizations. In fact, the superstitious, conceptualizing mind cannot count the realizations brought by inner fire. It is the secret key that opens you to *all* realizations.

Even if you could stay in samadhi meditation twenty-four hours a day for twenty days, Milarepa would say to you, "That means nothing! It does not compare to my inner fire meditation." This is how he responded to Gampopa at their first meeting, after Gampopa had described his meditation experiences. There must have been a reason for Milarepa to say this. He was not just making propaganda, exaggerating the power of inner fire. He had no partiality and had given up all worldly competition. Milarepa was simply saying that even remaining for many days in a deep, undisturbed samadhi meditation is nothing when compared to inner fire meditation. Inner fire is incomparable.

Personally, I like inner fire meditation. I don't claim to have any realizations, but I have tried it and I am convinced. Inner fire meditation will absolutely convince you too. It will change your entire notion of reality. You will come to trust the tantric path through this meditation.

We really need tantra these days because there is a tremendous explosion of delusion and distraction. Good things are happening in our lives, but many bad things are happening too, and we need the atomic energy of inner fire to blast us out of our confusion. In fact, without tantric practice, enlightenment is not possible.

In the beginning your inner fire meditation might not be successful. You might even have a negative reaction, such as an explosion of heat that drenches your body with sweat. However, I believe that even an imperfect result like this is still significant because it shows you the power of your mind.

It is said that anybody can do inner fire meditation. If you have never done it before, it might seem difficult, but it is actually simple. "How can I meditate like this?" you might think. "I am not a great meditator. In any case, I have created so much negative karma—how can I do advanced practices like these?" You should not think this way! You never know what you can do; you cannot always see your own potential. Perhaps you were a great meditator in a previous life. Right now your mind might be completely distracted, but one day your potential will suddenly ripen, and you will be able to meditate.

Look at Milarepa. I doubt that you have created more negative karma than he did; he killed many people when he was young. But because of his inner strength, he was also able to develop perfect renunciation, perfect bodhicitta, perfect right view, perfect Six Yogas of Naropa. He said good-bye to samsara.

Milarepa is a good example for us. Look around in the world. Sometimes those who are successful at samsara, who create strong negativity, can also be successful at liberation. On the other hand, those who don't have success at samsara can't be successful at liberation either.

My point is that you never know what human beings can do. Be brave! Try as much as possible to do the inner fire meditation. Even if you are not completely successful, at least you will gain some experience, and that is good enough.

Let us dedicate our energy to all universal living beings, praying that they actualize the essence of tantra and discover the union of their own unsurpassed bliss and nonduality wisdom.

Dedication is important; it is not just a Tibetan ritual. Having created an atmosphere of positive energy within our minds, we make the determination to share it with others.

Think, "Now, and for the rest of my life, I will enjoy myself as much as possible and try to create a good situation around me by giving to others the best part of my divine qualities and blissful energy. May this joyful present lead to unsurpassed joyful realizations in the future."

2. The Six Yogas and the Mahasiddha Naropa

The Six Yogas of Naropa were not discovered by Naropa. They originated in the teachings of Lord Buddha and were eventually transmitted to the great eleventh-century Indian yogi Tilopa, who in turn transmitted them to his disciple Naropa. They were then passed on to many Tibetan lamas, including Marpa and Milarepa, some of whom wrote down their experiences as commentaries on the Six Yogas.

I will be explaining the practice of inner fire according to *Having the Three Convictions,* a commentary on the Six Yogas by Lama Je Tsongkhapa. I will not translate the entire text, but will instead give you the essence of the teaching. Even though I am not a successful meditator, I have received teachings on this text from my gurus on at least three occasions,[1] and I have tried to do the practice.

As I have already mentioned, Lama Tsongkhapa lists the Six Yogas as inner fire meditation, the yoga of the illusory body, the yoga of clear light, transference of consciousness, transference into another body, and the yoga of the intermediate state. Lama Tsongkhapa explains the subjects without adding or subtracting anything. He says that all the subjects are covered by these six topics and that anybody who expects additional meditations is ignorant of the tradition. What does he mean? I think Lama Tsongkhapa means that to teach something from your own experience that is not contained in these six subjects is foolish. It would be like Tibetans boasting that they can make better pizzas than Italians.

Sometimes the subjects of the Six Yogas of Naropa are classified into two, three, four, or even ten divisions. In accordance with the needs of a meditator's mind, for example, there can be three divisions:

the practices for attaining enlightenment in this life, in the intermediate state, and in a future life. Or there can be two divisions: the
actual completion stage meditation subjects and the cooperative causes
for developing them. For example, some of the breathing exercises are
not formally part of completion stage practice, but they help the completion stage meditations.

Previously, some lamas were interested only in the actual completion stage meditations and did not explain these cooperative methods.
The holders of Marpa's lineages,[2] however, explain the various minor
techniques that are needed to help you succeed in completion stage
yoga. For inner fire meditation alone, Marpa explained hundreds of
technical methods.

Some Kagyu texts on the Six Yogas of Naropa, explaining according to Marpa's heritage, count six subjects: inner fire meditation, illusory body yoga, dream yoga, clear light yoga, intermediate state yoga,
and the yoga of transference of consciousness. Other Kagyu lamas list
eight yogas, adding evolutionary stage yoga and consort practice to
these six. Milarepa divides the six yogas differently: evolutionary stage
yoga, inner fire meditation, consort practice, clear light yoga, illusory
body yoga, and dream yoga. There are many different ways to count
the yogas.

Some Tibetan texts question whether all the Six Yogas of Naropa
actually come from Naropa. It seems that in Naropa's time there
might have been six separate texts and that some of Naropa's disciples
might have later combined the six. This might or might not be true,
but it doesn't really matter. History is always debatable. As long as we
are able to taste the chocolate of this practice, who cares about such
academic questions?

The Tibetan title of Lama Tsongkhapa's text is *Yi-che sum den,*
which I translate as *Having the Three Convictions. Yi-che* means conviction, which implies that you can have confidence; *sum* means
three; and *den* means having. In other words, this commentary has
three distinguishing characteristics. The first is that Lama
Tsongkhapa's descriptions of the meditations are clean-clear and
integrated. The second is that although there are many subjects, each
is presented so distinctly and clearly that it can be comprehended

easily by anyone with discriminating wisdom. The third characteristic is that in order to prove his points, Lama Tsongkhapa quotes many scriptures, both the tantric texts of Shakyamuni Buddha and the treatises of many of the lineage lamas.

Lama Tsongkhapa takes great care to base each of his statements on the words of lineage lamas such as Tilopa, Naropa, Marpa, and Milarepa. He uses quotations to show how his explanations are linked to theirs and to demonstrate the long history of these teachings. He gives clear, scientific explanations and uses convincing proofs on every subject. Thus we can have confidence in Lama Je Tsongkhapa's commentary.

In Tibetan, the Six Yogas of Naropa are called *Na-ro chö druk. Na-ro* refers to Naropa; *chö,* which means dharma, can refer to doctrine or phenomena; and *druk* means six. Some people have translated *Na-ro chö druk* as "The Six Doctrines of Naropa"; others as "The Six Yogas of Naropa." My feeling is that although "The Six Doctrines" is literally correct, it gives the impression that the teachings are purely philosophical or theological. They are not. They are something very practical, something to be actualized right now. I believe that "The Six Yogas of Naropa" conveys the right meaning, the right feeling. I think Naropa would be unhappy if we were to use the term "The Six Doctrines of Naropa."

I have reasons for saying that Naropa would be unhappy if we were to regard his Six Yogas as purely philosophical. Naropa was a well-educated monk and the top professor at the ancient Indian Buddhist university of Nalanda. With a mind like a computer, he had vast knowledge of the sutras and tantras. He was famous as an expert debater and was able to defeat all the non-Buddhist scholars in public encounters.

Nevertheless, Naropa was unhappy and dissatisfied and longed for realization. He thought to himself, "There's something wrong. I have learned all these intellectual ideas and I can explain absolutely everything about the Buddhadharma, yet I still feel empty and dissatisfied. Something is missing."

Naropa's guru instructed him to recite one of Heruka's mantras, *oṃ hrīḥ hā hā hūṃ hūṃ phaṭ,* until he found a solution to his problem. Naropa recited several million mantras. Then one day, while reciting the mantra, he felt the earth shake. A voice spoke to him from space, "You are still a baby! You have a long way to go. Your knowledge is merely intellectual, and this is not enough. In order to gain real satisfaction you must find Tilopa. He is your special guru."

So Naropa left the monastery in search of Tilopa. When he eventually found him after months of difficulties, Tilopa was sitting on the ground cooking live fish. He looked more like a madman than a great yogi! Nevertheless, Naropa became Tilopa's disciple. Year after year Naropa requested his guru for initiation; and year after year Tilopa would get him to perform some outrageous action, always denying him the initiation he so desperately wanted. Naropa struggled like this for twelve years, and twelve times he almost died.

One day while they were walking together in the desert, Tilopa suddenly decided to give Naropa the initiation. Unable to make any other preparations, Naropa mixed his urine with sand and offered this to his guru as a mandala. Then *pam*! Tilopa beat him on the head with his sandal. Naropa went into deep meditation for seven days.

It is good for us to hear this story of Naropa. These days we have no shortage of intellectual information, but I truly believe there is a shortage of *fertilization*. We collect so much information, but we do very little with it. This is why we have so little success in our spiritual practice. Many of my older students, for example, have heard the lam-rim twenty or thirty times and know everything about it from beginning to end. Yet still they are dissatisfied.

This is why Naropa is a good example for us. Even though he was highly advanced intellectually, he had not discovered satisfaction within himself. He left Nalanda in search of a tantric master and then struggled for all those years. He practiced continuously until he achieved his goal, enlightenment.

3. The Mahasiddha Je Tsongkhapa

In the Western academic world, the common interpretation is that Lama Je Tsongkhapa was just a philosopher. Western academics do not seem to recognize him as a great yogi, a great tantric practitioner, a mahasiddha. Actually, Lama Tsongkhapa taught and wrote more on tantra than on sutra; but because he did not publicly show his mahasiddha aspect, Westerners have the impression that he was merely an intellectual.[1]

Some people think that Gelugpas, the followers of Lama Tsongkhapa, do not practice nonconceptual meditation. They think that the other traditions of Tibetan Buddhism meditate in this way, but that Lama Tsongkhapa negated nonconceptual meditation and taught only intellectual, analytical meditation. I have heard Westerners say, "Gelugpas are always intellectualizing, always squeezing their brains." This is not true.

Lama Tsongkhapa was already a great meditator while still a teenager. From then on, he did not experience ordinary sicknesses; when he had a small health problem, he would cure himself. Also, if a flood or an avalanche was about to happen, he would say a prayer, and the disaster would be averted. If you read Lama Tsongkhapa's biography, you will see that he was a great mahasiddha.

Mönlam Chenmo, the great prayer festival celebrated in Lhasa for the two weeks after the Tibetan New Year, was started by Lama Je Tsongkhapa.[2] The monks, nuns, and laypeople of all the traditions of Tibetan Buddhism came together to make offerings, including thousands of butterlamps, and to say prayers. One day during the first festival, the many thousands of butterlamps in the temple became one huge mass of flame. The fire was soon out of control. Terrified that the temple might burn down, people ran to Lama Tsongkhapa for help. He sat down, went into deep samadhi meditation, and suddenly all the flames were extinguished, as if blown out by one gust of wind.

Lama Tsongkhapa was able to do this through his inner fire meditation. We Tibetans believe that when you can control the four elements of your own nervous system through inner fire meditation, you can also control the external elements. Lama Tsongkhapa didn't need an ordinary fire engine; with his inner fire engine, he instantly extinguished the flames. This proves that Lama Tsongkhapa was a powerful realized being. At that time he also had visions of the Eighty-four Mahasiddhas, perceiving them in the skies above Lhasa.

Lama Tsongkhapa also had no shortage of telepathic power. For example, he was once staying in a small retreat hut some thirty minutes' walk from the place where he later advised Sera Monastery be built. Suddenly one day he disappeared, and nobody knew why. Later that same day a delegation from the Emperor of China arrived; the Emperor had heard of Lama Tsongkhapa's fame and wished to invite him to come to China, but he was nowhere to be found. No one knew the delegation was coming that day, but Lama Tsongkhapa knew, and he escaped over the mountains.

This shows Lama Tsongkhapa's telepathic power, but it is also a good example of his perfect renunciation. He vomited at the thought of worldly pleasure. Can you imagine us in that situation? We would definitely accept the invitation. I can't even resist an invitation to visit a rich benefactor, let alone an emperor. Although Lama Tsongkhapa was incredibly famous, he never went to distracting places but preferred to stay in isolated places in the mountains. On the other hand, we go to the most confused places, which shows that our renunciation is not yet perfect.

Lama Je Tsongkhapa had many thousands of disciples all over Tibet and constantly received offerings, but he had no bank account, no house, and not even one piece of land on which to grow his food. He gave away everything he received and stayed clean-clear. Lama Tsongkhapa was the head of Ganden, a monastery he founded, but he stayed there as if he were simply a guest: he would arrive, receive offerings, give them away, then leave with nothing. Lama Tsongkhapa is a perfect example of someone living in accordance with Dharma.

Lama Tsongkhapa's death also reveals that he was a mahasiddha. From his childhood, Lama Tsongkhapa had a special relationship with the Buddha Manjushri and received teachings directly from Manjushri. Two or three years before Lama Tsongkhapa died, Manjushri told him that he was about to die. Suddenly countless Buddhas appeared. They requested Lama Tsongkhapa not to die and gave him an initiation of boundless energy so that he could live longer. Manjushri then told him that his life span had been extended and predicted the new time of his death.

Shortly before Lama Tsongkhapa died, one of his teeth fell out, and everybody saw that it emitted rainbow light. He gave the tooth to Khedrub Je, one of his heart sons, but this disappointed his other disciples, who asked if they could have some of the tooth. Lama Tsongkhapa told Khedrub Je to place the tooth in a box on the altar, where radiant rainbow light continued to emanate from it, and everyone prayed and meditated.

A week later, when Lama Tsongkhapa opened the box, the tooth had transformed into a tiny Tara image surrounded by relic pills. Lama Tsongkhapa gave the Tara statue to Khedrub Je and the relic pills to the other disciples. He also predicted that after five hundred years the relics would be brought to Bodhgaya in India. This prediction was accurate. Although the Chinese Communists destroyed what remained of Lama Je Tsongkhapa's body, some of the relics were saved and taken to Bodhgaya by Tibetans fleeing into exile in India.

When Lama Tsongkhapa finally died, he died perfectly. First, he put everything in order. Next, he asked one of his disciples to bring him his skullcup. He then performed the inner offering meditation and took thirty-three sips of the inner offering, a sign that inside he was the Guhyasamaja deity.[3] Finally, sitting in meditation in his full robes, he died. These are the actions that distinguish a mahasiddha from an ordinary being. An accomplished master doesn't have to announce, "I am a mahasiddha." His actions prove it.

Can you imagine being able to die deliberately and clean-clear?

When we die, we leave a mess. We should motivate and pray that instead of dying like a cow, we will die as Lama Je Tsongkhapa did. This is our human right. Pray that instead of dying in a depressed, miserable state, you will die blissfully. Make the resolution, "When I die, I will control my emotions and die peacefully, just as Lama Tsongkhapa did." You must motivate, because motivation has power. When the time of your death comes, you will remember your resolution. On the other hand, if you don't have strong motivation now, you will end up shaking with terror and completely lose control when your death comes. If you have prepared yourself beforehand, you will remember what to do at the time of death.

At one point after Lama Je Tsongkhapa had passed away, Khedrub Je was sad because he felt that Lama Tsongkhapa's teachings were disappearing. Lama Tsongkhapa had explained the entire path to enlightenment thoroughly from beginning to end, from Hinayana to Paramitayana and Tantrayana, and thousands upon thousands of people had meditated upon his teachings and achieved realizations. However, Khedrub Je thought, "Lama Je Tsongkhapa's teachings seem like a mirage. Unfortunately the Tibetan people are degenerating. He taught us not to cling to the desires of the sensory world, yet people have more grasping and more desires than ever."

Khedrub Je felt very sad, and he cried and cried. He then prayed and offered a mandala. Suddenly Lama Tsongkhapa appeared to him in a vision. He was in a youthful aspect, seated on a jeweled throne surrounded by deities, dakas, and dakinis. He said to Khedrub Je, "My son, you shouldn't cry. My principal message is to practice the tantric path. Do this and then transmit the teachings to qualified disciples. Instead of crying you should help to do this as much as possible, and you will make me very happy."

At another time, Khedrub Je had some technical questions on tantric practice but could not find anyone who could answer them. Again he burst into tears. His heart was breaking. When he prayed strongly and offered a mandala, Lama Je Tsongkhapa again manifested to him in a vision and gave him many teachings and initiations.

At yet another time that Khedrub Je cried so hard and prayed so much, Lama Tsongkhapa manifested to him in the aspect of a mahasiddha. Reddish in color, he was holding a sword and a skullcup and riding on a tiger. He also manifested to Khedrub Je in the form of Manjushri, and at another time in his usual form, but riding on a white elephant. Five visions appeared when, for different reasons, Khedrub Je cried and prayed to Lama Tsongkhapa.

Why do I tell these stories? It is inspiring to know that Lama Je Tsongkhapa was without doubt a great yogi, a mahasiddha, and that Khedrub Je had such inner realizations that Lama Tsongkhapa would manifest when Khedrub Je simply called on him. You should also understand that Lama Tsongkhapa's principal field was tantra. Even though we are degenerate, we are very fortunate to have the chance to hear Lama Tsongkhapa's way of explaining the tantric path and to try to actualize it. Even if we do not know very much about Buddhist teachings, if we practice what we do know, Lama Tsongkhapa will be very happy with us.

4. The Point Is to Practice

It is good to think about the lives of mahasiddhas such as Naropa and Lama Je Tsongkhapa so that you know how you have to practice. Even after you have learned lam-rim, there are still times when you are unclear about what you have to do. When you look at the lifestyles of the mahasiddhas, many things become clear.

We can see from their biographies that intellectual knowledge of Dharma alone is not enough—we have to practice. There are many stories of learned Dharma scholars having to ask for guidance from people who have not studied any of the vast treatises but who have really tasted the few teachings they have received. I remember Kyabje Trijang Rinpoche, the Junior Tutor to His Holiness the Dalai Lama, saying in his teachings that when it comes to practice, many intellectuals have to go to beggars on the street to ask for advice. Even though these scholars may have intellectually learned the entire sutra and tantra teachings and may even teach them to many students, they are still empty when it comes to practice.

Rinpoche was saying that this is happening in the Tibetan community, but it is good for us, too, to keep his words in mind. Can you imagine spending twenty or thirty years studying the Dharma and still not improving within yourself, still not even knowing how to begin to practice? You might think that this is not possible, yet it can happen.

The Six Yogas of Naropa are not something philosophical. You have to act, so that some inner transformation takes place. The teachings must become real for you. Take karma, for instance. When we talk about karma, we intellectualize so much. We need to come down to earth. Karma is not something complicated or philosophical.

Karma means watching your body, watching your mouth, and watching your mind. Trying to keep these three doors as pure as possible is the practice of karma.

There are many monks leading ascetic lives in Dharamsala in India, where His Holiness the Dalai Lama lives. Even though they are perhaps not very learned, they spend many years meditating and doing retreat in small huts on the mountainsides. On the other hand, there are other very learned monks who do not want to live ascetic lives. Those living in retreat on the mountain really try to taste the Dharma, and I think they succeed. They taste the chocolate, while the famous scholars miss out. In the end, it doesn't matter who you are; if you want to taste something, you have to go to the taste-place.

It is exactly the same in the West. Many people easily gain an incredible intellectual understanding of Buddhism, but it is a dry understanding that does not fertilize the heart. There are some Western professors, for example, who have studied Buddhism for years. They have high degrees in Buddhist studies and have published books on the sutras and tantras. Yet many of them admit that they are not even Buddhists, which means they haven't actualized what they write about. They can read Lama Je Tsongkhapa's texts and translate them using incredible words, but for them it remains mere theory. I find this shocking.

On the other hand, some people have heard just a few lam-rim teachings, such as the workings of the negative mind, but they begin to look inside themselves and to meditate. The teachings gradually become part of them. The mere intellectuals, however, think that the negative mind is somewhere else—up on top of Mount Everest, perhaps. They don't care about the negative mind because they think that it doesn't refer to them.

Many of my students who are interested in learning more about Dharma ask me whether they should learn Tibetan. I say to them, "If you want to learn Tibetan, learn it. If you don't want to learn it, don't. There is plenty of information available in English and other languages." I have my reasons for answering them in this way. I'm sympathetic to Western students, and I've been watching them for many years. Many of my students have learned Tibetan, but after they have learned it, some of them seem to practice Dharma less. This doesn't make sense to me. Tibetan is not a holy language. In every culture you learn a language—it's part of samsara. In learning Tibetan, you learn a Tibetan samsaric trip. This is why I am not very interested in my students learning Tibetan. The important point is to taste the chocolate. No matter how small a piece you get, as long as you taste it, you will be satisfied.

I remember something His Holiness the Dalai Lama said during a commentary on the Six Yogas of Naropa. He described his visit to some Kagyu monasteries, where he saw many monks who were not especially learned but who were practicing very seriously in retreat, leading ascetic lives and undergoing many hardships. These monks studied a small part of a commentary, then immediately put great energy and effort into meditating on it. His Holiness said that, on the other hand, some Gelugpa monks are very learned but do not put much energy into their practice. His Holiness expressed the wish for there to be a balance between those who have not learned much yet put incredible energy into practicing meditation and those who are incredibly learned yet do very little meditation practice. I am sure His Holiness was not joking, nor was he being sectarian. He was impressed by the Kagyu retreatants.

My point is that as soon as you clearly understand a subject, you should hold it in your heart and practice it. You will then taste the teaching. For example, once someone has shown you exactly how to make pizza—how to combine the tomatoes, the mozzarella cheese, the herbs, and so forth—that is enough for you to make pizza and to eat it. However, Western people are easily confused. If someone comes along and says to you, "Oh, you don't know much! You can't make pizza because you don't know how to make curry," you will think that you can't cook at all.

Of course, I am not saying that you should not learn Dharma well; but take whatever you learn into your heart and integrate it. In fact, according to the great Sakya Pandita, someone who tries to meditate without first receiving the teachings is like a person without arms or legs trying to climb up a steep mountain. This means that if you don't first get the information about how to make a pizza, trying to make a pizza will be a disaster. But it is nonsense to say that people who don't know how to make a curry cannot make a pizza. Many people make this same mistake with Dharma.

There are other misconceptions. For example, Lama Je Tsongkhapa has said that first we should study extensively, next we should understand how to practice the teachings, and then we should practice day and night. We might interpret the words "first this, second this, third this" to mean that we have to study for thirty or forty years before we even start to meditate. Such misconceptions do exist.

Suppose I ask one of my students how long he has studied Buddhadharma, and he answers, "Ten years." I then say to him, "Ten years? Ten years' study means nothing. In order to be able to practice you have to study at least thirty or forty years, because first you have to study for a long time, then you have to reflect on everything, and finally you have to practice day and night. Lama Je Tsongkhapa said so." It is easy to be misled in this way.

Understanding the three negativities of body, the four of speech, and the three of mind is enough for you to learn to avoid them.[1] We don't need to learn the entire sutra and tantra teachings in order to practice the opposite of these, the ten virtuous actions. It is essential that we bring the correct understanding of Buddhism into the Western world, not one bound by cultural chains. When everything is clean-clear in your own mind, nobody can create obstacles for you.

When Lama Tsongkhapa was still a teenager, he did a Manjushri retreat. Relatively speaking, he had not yet studied much, but he went into retreat and had many meditation experiences. Lama Tsongkhapa's way of practicing unified listening, analytical checking, and meditation, and it also unified sutra and tantra.

It is important to have a firm practice. Students who have listened to Dharma teachings for many years sometimes say, "I am confused! I don't know where to start. I've received so many teachings from so many lamas, but I still don't know who my real teacher is or what meditations to do." Even though these students have studied many subjects and have learned a hundred meditation techniques, they are still lost. This shows that something is wrong.

The beauty of Tibetan Buddhism is that it has a clear structure from beginning to end. Perhaps you find all these outlines boring, but Tibetan Buddhism is alive today because of its clear structure. All four traditions have a clean-clear approach, and this should be much appreciated. If ten steps are involved in going from here to there but some of the information is missing, you cannot go all the way. If you have a clear map, however, you won't get lost.

Since we are gaining a Buddhist education, we should be aware of what we need and what we lack. To some extent, you do know what you need. When you are hungry, you recognize the fact and search for food. When you are thirsty, you know that drinking something will solve your problem. In the same way, when you feel any kind of dissatisfaction, simply try to solve the problem. Deal with the gross problems first, then gradually the more subtle ones. Be practical. Use your inner wisdom—and just act!

Try to be reasonable in the way you grow, and don't ever think it is too late. It is never too late. Even if you are going to die tomorrow, keep yourself straight and clear and be a happy human being today. If you keep your situation happy day by day, you will eventually reach the greatest happiness of enlightenment.

Remember, we are all responsible for our own lives. Don't think that this Tibetan monk will give you enlightenment or make you powerful. It is not like that. Just think, "At this time in my life I have come into contact with this monk, and I will judge him realistically. I will not blindly accept what he says but will check up on whether it is right or wrong and debate with him."

Anyone who claims to be a Buddhist knows that the principal concern of Buddhism is the mind. The mind is the nucleus of samsara and nirvana. Every experience we have in our lives manifests from our mind. Because you interpret your life and your world through your mental attitude, it is important to have the right motivation. Wrong motivation brings pain, disappointment, and extremes in life. Think in this way, "During the rest of my life, it is my responsibility to grow in mindfulness and happiness. Each day I will expand the loving kindness I already have. When I wake up each morning, I will open my wisdom-eye and see more and more deeply into the inner universal reality. I will try to be as mindful as possible. I will take responsibility for my life and dedicate it to others by growing strong in loving kindness and wisdom. I will serve others as much as possible." Make the determination that this will be your way of life.

PART TWO

Preliminary Practices

5. Preparing the Mind

Lama Je Tsongkhapa's commentary *Having the Three Convictions* is divided into two major sections: the preliminaries and the main practices. The preliminaries themselves are also divided into two: the common and the uncommon preliminary practices.[1]

❧ THE COMMON PRELIMINARIES

The common Mahayana preliminaries are all of the lam-rim meditations, such as those on the value of human life, renunciation, refuge, loving kindness, bodhicitta, emptiness, and so forth.

Lama Tsongkhapa explains that in order to actualize the Six Yogas of Naropa, we must first practice all these meditations. He later adds, however, that he will not give details here of the common preliminaries because he has already written extensively about them in his lam-rim texts.[2]

Lama Tsongkhapa points out that all the lineage lamas advised their disciples to practice the common Mahayana preliminaries before doing tantric practice. He shows this by using quotations from Marpa, Milarepa, Gampopa, and Pagmo Drupa. Even though the preliminaries are sometimes not mentioned as part of the Six Yogas, these great masters always taught them before giving actual instructions on the Six Yogas. Failing to prepare the mind in this way would be like putting too much luggage on a yak; when the yak falls down the mountain, both the yak and the luggage are lost. Also, as Milarepa put it, when the guru does not teach in the right way, both the guru and disciple will fall over the precipice of disaster, like two yaks yoked together.

We can clearly see from Lama Tsongkhapa's writing that he is non-sectarian. This commentary, with its many quotations from early Kagyu masters such as Milarepa and Gampopa, shows his extensive research into the other traditions. If the advice is correct, Lama Tsongkhapa doesn't care who gives it. Egotistical teachers praise their own tradition and have nothing good to say about the other orders of Tibetan Buddhism. Lama Tsongkhapa, however, shows great respect for the Kagyu tradition.

Lama Tsongkhapa, the founder of the Gelugpa order, had the opportunity to write about the Six Yogas of Naropa because of the kindness of the early Kagyu masters. If lamas such as Marpa and Milarepa had not transmitted these teachings, Lama Tsongkhapa would not have known about them, and we also would not have the opportunity to practice them.

Lama Tsongkhapa emphasizes that the preliminaries are very powerful and that our practice will not be stable unless we do them. He says that if we don't cut the ego-games of this life, we cannot have stable Dharma practice. If we don't have devotion that goes beyond our mouth, taking refuge is meaningless. If we don't comprehend karma, taking protective vows is a joke. If we haven't developed renunciation, seeking liberation is useless. If we don't have loving kindness, calling ourselves Mahayanists is empty talk. And if we don't have the strong will to practice the six perfections of a bodhisattva, our bodhi-sattva ordination is also a joke.

This is simply lam-rim: saying things in a different way sometimes brings comprehension. Lama Je Tsongkhapa quotes Lama Atisha and Milarepa extensively on this point about not doing Mickey Mouse practice.

❧ THE UNCOMMON PRELIMINARIES

The uncommon, or tantric, preliminaries also have two divisions: the general preliminaries and the specific tantric preliminaries, or *ngöndro*. The general preliminaries are receiving an initiation (see chapter 6) and observing the ethics of the bodhisattva and tantric vows, or *samaya*. In the Gelug tradition there are nine specific tantric preliminaries, but Lama Tsongkhapa mentions only three[3]—mandala offerings, Vajrasattva practice, and guru yoga—and discusses in detail only the last two (see chapters 7 and 8) because they are emphasized in the teachings of the lineage lamas of the Six Yogas of Naropa. Lama Tsongkhapa also points out that once we have established the preliminaries, we need to meditate on evolutionary stage yoga in order to become qualified for the completion stage practices of the Six Yogas (see chapters 9 and 10).

In *Having the Three Convictions*, Lama Tsongkhapa pays considerable attention to the tantric preliminaries. We should perform one hundred thousand of each of the tantric preliminaries, but I don't think this always happens nowadays. In Lama Tsongkhapa's time, I think his followers did the preliminaries as he advised. My assumption, however, is that later some Gelugpas thought, "These preliminary practices with their hundreds of thousands of mandala offerings, water-bowl offerings, prostrations, guru yoga, and Vajrasattva mantras are for people who are not intelligent. They need this kind of preparation, but an intelligent person like me doesn't."

It is possible that you too may become proud in this way, making some fantastic, elegant statement about being a great meditator and that prostrations are for people with no brains. This view is completely wrong.

Also, you should not imagine that doing these preliminaries intensively is exclusively a Kagyu or Nyingma tradition and that Gelugpas don't need to do them. This is a wrong impression. All Tibetan traditions say that you must do the seven-limb practice,[4] so how can you give up prostrations?

Some Gelug texts say that the most important preliminary is meditation on the three principal paths—renunciation, bodhicitta, and emptiness—and that the other preliminaries are secondary. You might interpret this to mean that you don't need to do the preliminary sets of prostrations and so forth, but this would be a mistake.

Lama Tsongkhapa was a realized being, yet he still did prostrations. In fact, he did so many that his body made an impression in solid rock. The mark left by his body is still visible at his hermitage in Tibet. While doing the prostrations, he had a divine vision of the

Thirty-five Buddhas of Confession. This shows how powerful these preliminary practices are.

It is good to practice these tantric preliminaries on a daily basis, but doing a little every day is not enough. In order to experience their power, it is necessary sometimes to do these practices intensively in retreat, just as Lama Tsongkhapa did. It is a profoundly different experience.

Now, let's offer a dedication. "May I and all mother sentient beings develop perfect renunciation, perfect loving kindness and bodhicitta, and perfect wisdom of emptiness, and thereby be qualified to practice inner fire meditation and attain mahasiddha realizations, just as Naropa and Je Tsongkhapa did."

6. Receiving Initiation

The first of the general uncommon preliminaries, as I have mentioned, is receiving tantric initiation. To practice the Six Yogas of Naropa, we need to receive the four complete initiations—vase, secret, wisdom, and word—of a great initiation of Highest Yoga Tantra. Merely receiving an oral transmission of a practice is not sufficient. Since the Six Yogas of Naropa are closely connected with Heruka Chakrasamvara and Hevajra, they are the best initiations to receive.

Lama Je Tsongkhapa mentions that before giving Gampopa teachings on the Six Yogas, Milarepa asked him, "Have you received initiation?" When Gampopa replied that he had, Milarepa gave him the commentary. Lama Tsongkhapa cites here another quotation from an ancient tantric text, *The Diamond Rosary Tantra*, which says that initiation is essential, that it is the root of realizations, and that receiving tantric teachings without an initiation causes both the teacher and the disciple to go to the lower realms. By showing that all the great lineage gurus advised their disciples to first receive initiation, Lama Tsongkhapa proves that initiation is a necessary preliminary to the Six Yogas of Naropa.

What is initiation? It is the beginning of the experience of meditation and concentration, of penetration into the nature of the reality of all phenomena. Initiation leads us into the mandala of a deity and into the totality of the experience of that deity. It is an antidote to the dissatisfied, samsaric, fanatical, dualistic mind. During initiation we should completely let go of our preconceptions and fixed ideas of who we are, of our limited self-image. Instead, we need to identify with the wisdom-mind of the deity, which is our own perfect potential.

The tantric teachings place much emphasis on great bliss as the basis of the initiation experience. Of course, if you don't have blissful experiences in your daily life, it will be difficult to experience bliss in your meditation—but we all experience happiness and bliss to some extent. The tantric teachings show us how to work with and expand our natural physical and mental resources of pleasure, and eventually how to unify bliss with the wisdom that understands emptiness and achieve liberation.

Initiation does not mean that a guru gives you some incredible power. You already *have* the qualities of profound wisdom and great bliss within you; initiation simply activates them.

The quality of the initiation you receive does not depend on the guru. It depends on you. The lama giving the initiation must have received the lineage of the initiation and done the basic retreats, but the important point is the disciple's attitude. If you are motivated by the sincere wish to transform yourself so that you will be able to benefit others, you should receive the initiation.

It is important to have a dedicated attitude. In fact, according to Buddhist psychology, unless you dedicate yourself to others, you will never be satisfied. Instead you will be bored and lonely. It is logical that dedication to others brings you the satisfaction that you crave. To receive an initiation in order to achieve some kind of power for your own ego is not good; but to do so in order to dedicate yourself to others and thereby achieve something for yourself is totally appropriate.

You should visualize that you are receiving the initiation not from an ordinary human being but from the mandala deity. During a Heruka Chakrasamvara initiation, for example, you should see the lama as Guru Heruka, with a body of infinitely blue, radiant light.

Even though a hundred people might participate in an initiation, they do not all have the same experience. Each person experiences the initiation according to their own level of skill and personal development. Actually receiving the initiation depends on the person's mind, not on their bodily participation. As I mentioned, it depends on their ability to let go of their limited self-image.

Initiation is a serious business. Naropa had to wait twelve years and perform outrageous feats before Tilopa would give him an initiation.

In ancient times initiation would not be given in public to large groups of people as they often are nowadays. Only a few people would be allowed to attend at one time. And the four initiations would not be given all at once as they are now. Disciples would receive the first part, then go away and digest it. When they had reached that particular level in their practice, they would then come back to receive the next level of the initiation. It is much easier for us to receive initiation nowadays.

Lama Tsongkhapa emphasizes that during initiation we should go slowly: penetrating, meditating, concentrating. We shouldn't be too concerned if our meditation during an initiation seems to be only at the level of imagination and not the actual experience. Simply imagining the experience plants seeds in the field of our consciousness, and these seeds will slowly grow. It is just like the story of the hamburger: first someone had to imagine it, then gradually it manifested in the American culture.

As you come to understand the process of tantric initiation, you will discover the real meaning of tantra. The initiation process, in fact, embodies the actual experience of the stages of tantric realization, from the beginning right up to the stage of mahasiddha attainment. The vase initiation emphasizes evolutionary yoga practice, the secret initiation emphasizes the illusory body, the wisdom initiation emphasizes clear light wisdom, and the word empowerment emphasizes the unity of the fully developed illusory body and clear light. The Six Yogas of Naropa explain exactly how to approach this realization of the word empowerment, which is the experience of full enlightenment.

At the end of an initiation, you should feel that you have become enlightened, and you should make the determination, "From now on I will not project the hallucinations and concrete conceptions of my self-pity mind, the source of misery. Instead, I will identify with my divine wisdom-energy, the source of pleasure, and offer this to all living beings."

As long as we maintain mindfulness and don't lose control, it doesn't matter how much blissful pleasure we experience. With the right attitude, our pleasure becomes our liberation.

7. Purifying Negativities

In the view of tantra, attainment of higher realizations depends on first purifying negativities. There is no point in pushing your meditation until you have done something to lessen the obstacles to realization. I think you often push too much. You complain, "I meditate and meditate, but my meditation never improves." This happens because you have not yet created the right conditions for realizations. You need to do powerful purification practices, such as the Vajrasattva meditation and mantra recitation, which is one of the tantric preliminaries described in detail in *Having the Three Convictions*.

Vajrasattva is the manifestation of the purity of all the Buddhas. In general, Vajrasattva practice helps to improve both your meditation and your lifestyle. Meditate intensively on Vajrasattva whenever you experience problems in your life or have difficulty studying or practicing Dharma. You can sense when you need Vajrasattva practice. Even though you mightn't have single-pointed concentration, you will definitely experience some transformation by doing just three months of Vajrasattva retreat.

The Indian tantric text *The Essential Ornament* says that reciting twenty-one Vajrasattva mantras each day ensures that neither our natural negativities nor the negativities of breaking our tantric vows will increase. Broken tantric vows are the most serious obstacles to realizations, making the breaking of other vows seem insignificant. The text adds that reciting a hundred thousand Vajrasattva mantras can purify every negativity. Many of the lineage lamas say that doing a Vajrasattva retreat properly can purify even the breaking of all the tantric root vows.

You should utilize Vajrasattva practice as much as possible, especially if you have not done a full Vajrasattva retreat. You can combine Vajrasattva purification with the practice of inner fire, alternating them; they help each other. In this way you can complete the one hundred thousand Vajrasattva mantras while discovering the power of inner fire. Practicing the tantric preliminaries and completion stage together brings success. It is good for beginners to practice inner fire in the morning and to perform ten minutes of Vajrasattva purification in the evening before going to bed. You will then sleep comfortably, with a happy mind. If you go to sleep with a miserable mind, you will activate heavy karma all night.

The conventional, relative mind causes negativity to become bottled up and to increase. However, if you can recognize that even the concept of negative energy is an illusion and has the nature of nonduality, the negativity will be lessened. Just like everything else, positive and negative are interdependent; they are made up by our own mind.

Sometimes new Dharma students think, "Oh, no! So much talk about sin and negativity!" They think that God or Buddha created the negativity, but this is not true. Our own minds create the negative karma. We are the ones who think we are negative. As long as we consciously or unconsciously believe that we are impure, the self-pitying imagination will always be present, and we will then do self-pitying actions because we are emanating self-pitying vibrations. That's why purification is so important.

To purify means to psychologically work out our situation and our karma. The best way to do this is to realize the non-self-existence of negativity and of the self. Since this is difficult to understand, however, we need to do something about the psychological concepts that weigh us down. I firmly believe that negativity is shaken by reciting the hundred-syllable mantra of Vajrasattva even one time. I know it is powerful. Of course, there is a big difference between reciting a mantra correctly and incorrectly. We often recite mantras mindlessly. Reciting a hundred thousand mantras carelessly cannot be compared with reciting one mantra perfectly.

Lama Je Tsongkhapa describes the Vajrasattva meditation in detail in *Having the Three Convictions*, but I won't go into detail here as I have explained it elsewhere.[1] I will simply give you the essence of the practice.

Visualize Vajrasattva and his consort seated above your head on a lotus and moon seat. Their bodies are composed of radiant white light. Recognize the equal realizations of the male and female deities.

There are three ways to visualize the process of purification. With each visualization, you simultaneously recite the Vajrasattva mantra.

In the first technique, white nectar—like milk or liquid yogurt—flows forcefully down from the hearts of Vajrasattva and his consort. It comes down through their central channels to their joined lower chakras, then down through the lotus and moon seat. Like a powerful waterfall dropping from a great height, the nectar forcefully enters through the crown of your head and rushes down your central channel, completely purifying you. All your gross negative energy, your internal garbage, is forced out through the openings of your lower body in the form of snakes, scorpions, worms, ants, or whatever else you find effective. Alternatively, you could imagine the negativities coming out as roosters, pigs, and snakes, symbolic of the three poisonous minds of lust, ignorance, and hatred. All your gross negative energy is purified and disappears down into the earth.

In the second method, the blissful nectar coming from Vajrasattva and his consort pours down your central channel and fills you from your feet up to your crown. Visualize all your impure energy being forced up by the nectar and leaving your body through your nostrils and mouth, in much the same way that water poured into a dirty glass causes the rubbish in the glass to come to the top. This second technique is more subtle than the first.

The third technique involves light-energy rather than liquid. This powerful blissful light is white, but with a rainbow hue. It instantly shatters the darkness inside you. The darkness in your brain chakra, your throat chakra, your heart chakra, and everywhere else disappears without a trace. The nonfunctioning parts of your brain and nervous system are activated, and there is no space for impurities of body, speech, and mind. Your whole body becomes as transparent as crystal.

These three visualization techniques are the main meditations that accompany recitation of the Vajrasattva mantra. Since they bring results, you should practice them.

॥

Now, let us dedicate. "May there be no obstacles to our accomplishment of inner fire. May we all attain realizations in this life."

8. The Inspiration of the Guru

Guru yoga, the other tantric preliminary described in detail by Lama Tsongkhapa in *Having the Three Convictions,* is practiced to receive inspiration and blessings. It seems to be the most difficult practice for the Western mind, but it is really quite simple if you try to understand it in a rational way.

Shakyamuni Buddha revealed the tantras and other teachings two thousand five hundred years ago, but are these teachings real for you? He taught the Four Noble Truths, but is that enough for them to become truth for you? Shakyamuni Buddha, Naropa, Marpa, Milarepa, and Lama Je Tsongkhapa have already taught the essentials of the Six Yogas of Naropa, but without someone to introduce them to you, are they real for you? You may have books that explain exactly how to practice the Six Yogas of Naropa, but the results of following instructions from a book are questionable. Tantra is highly technical, internally technical, so a teacher is essential. Someone has to show you the practices so that they become an organic experience.

If you went to buy a Rolls-Royce and instead were given all the parts of the car and an instruction manual on how to assemble it, you would panic: "What's this? Where's my car?" You would need someone to show you how to put it together. It's the same here. We need someone to show us how to put everything together in our minds.

When our guru teaches us the Four Noble Truths, he gives us inspiration and blessings. He makes the Four Noble Truths real for us, so that they become our own realizations. Our wisdom that realizes the Four Noble Truths is the inspiration and blessing of the guru. When somebody shows you the Four Noble Truths and you then understand them, that in itself causes you to follow the path. This is logical and simple. It is not that the guru says, "I have shown you the Four Noble Truths; you must believe in them."

In this respect, I think the relationship between Western students and their teachers is better than that between Eastern students and their teachers, because no formal customs are involved. Westerners question everything, and I find this a very honest approach. If something does not make sense to you, you say so openly. If something makes sense to you, you say, "Yes, this is helpful. I will use it." There is no custom obliging you to answer or behave in a certain way. If you like or don't like something, you simply say so. This is very difficult for Eastern students to do, because they feel a social obligation to behave in a certain way. I feel the Western way is more realistic.

Because of the cultural differences, Tibetans sometimes don't understand the devotion of Western students, nor do Westerners understand the devotion of Tibetans. Different cultures have distinctly different perceptions.

I will give you an example of this. When my student Claudio is working as my attendant, he will casually ask me, "Lama, would you like some tea or coffee?" Tibetans would be shocked by Claudio's behavior. In Tibetan culture it is unacceptable for a student to approach his teacher so informally. The approach must be very respectful. But what is it all about? Only a cup of coffee! Whether the student behaves according to Tibetan or Western custom does not make it better coffee. It is just a cultural difference. Tibetans would say, "Look at the way that Italian student approaches his teacher! Western people have no humility or devotion." But the criticism is not really valid. It is illogical to say that Claudio is disrespectful simply because he behaves according to his culture.

When I first started to teach Westerners many years ago, most of my Tibetan friends were shocked. "How can you teach Westerners?" they asked. "How can they understand Buddhadharma? You are trying to do something that is impossible." Much negativity was directed at me.

As a matter of fact, it is more difficult to teach Western people than Tibetans. If Tibetans ask me whether they can purify all their negative karma by reciting the Vajrasattva mantra, I can simply answer by giving a relevant quotation from Shakyamuni Buddha or Lama Tsongkhapa. I don't have to think much about my answer. I can just cite some words from a text, and they will be satisfied. If you quote the right words, Tibetans will stay quiet. A Westerner, on the other hand, would demand, "Lama Je Tsongkhapa said what? Why did he say that? How can he say that? Does it work?" This is good; but because of the cultural differences, Tibetans are going to project that Westerners know very little about Dharma.

A few years ago, a learned Tibetan lama whom I had invited to teach at my Dharma center in England said to me, "Maybe you don't really need a highly qualified teacher for Western people. A simple one might be enough." He told me this quite seriously. I didn't say anything. There was no point in arguing with him since he had already accepted my invitation. He had to find out for himself.

I met him again six months later when I went to England to give teachings. I did not mention our previous conversation, but one day he commented to me, "What I said to you when I was in India was a mistake. I think it is very difficult to teach Westerners." This is an experiential report!

To meditate on guru yoga, visualize the essence of your guru manifesting in the space of nonduality in front of you in the form of Vajradhara. Guru Vajradhara sits on a lotus and sun seat on a throne supported by eight snow lions. He is radiant blue in color, holds a vajra and bell, and embraces a consort of the same color. Seeing their radiant blue light-bodies in space arouses great bliss and the wisdom of nonduality within you. Blue light and space automatically remind us of nonduality.

At their crown chakra is a moon seat with a white syllable *om* on it; at their throat chakra, a lotus seat with a red *āḥ;* and at their heart chakra, a sun seat with a blue *hūṃ.*

Think about Guru Vajradhara's great kindness and concern for you as explained in the lam-rim teachings. Although Guru Vajradhara is not your father or mother, not your husband or wife, not your boyfriend or girlfriend, he is still greatly concerned about your welfare. It is as though he exists solely for you.

Seeing the essence of Vajradhara as your own root guru brings a feeling of closeness, of personal kindness; and visualizing the guru in the aspect of Vajradhara brings inspiration and realizations quickly.

Light radiates from the *hūṃ* in Guru Vajradhara's heart into the ten directions. On each ray of light we can visualize one of the lineage lamas of the Six Yogas of Naropa, such as Tilopa, Naropa, Marpa, Milarepa, Gampopa, Pagmo Drupa, Butön, or Lama Je Tsongkhapa. These are the masters who practiced and achieved realization of inner fire and who discovered the totality of the illusory body and clear light wisdom.

When I visualize all these lineage gurus, I like to see each of them in the aspect of a mahasiddha. Mahasiddhas have vajra bodies vibrant with blissful kundalini energy. They have no desire for external objects because they have achieved perfect samadhi and simultaneously born wisdom. To see the lineage lamas in this way encourages and energizes us. Merely imagining them in this aspect causes tantalizing, blissful kundalini to flow in the central channel. Lama Tsongkhapa did not actually instruct us to visualize the lineage lamas in this way, but it does not contradict his advice. We should not think we cannot do something simply because it was not mentioned by Lama Tsongkhapa.

The usual way of depicting Lama Tsongkhapa, as a Buddhist monk, emphasizes his purity. In Tushita Pure Land, however, he has a different name and a different manifestation.[1] Also, I mentioned earlier Khedrub Je's five visions of Lama Tsongkhapa. In one of these Lama Tsongkhapa manifested as a mahasiddha riding on a tiger. I like to visualize him in this form.

As I mentioned earlier, Naropa was originally a monk at Nalanda Monastery; he was a superintelligent professor whom nobody could defeat in debate. Later, dissatisfied with this role and with mere intellectual knowledge, he went in search of Tilopa. After Naropa became Tilopa's disciple, Tilopa told him to give up dressing like a mahapandit. So Naropa took off his respectable robes and put on mahasiddha clothes, complete with a tiger skin. The professor became a wild-looking hippie.

Even though the Gelugpa tradition places strong emphasis on ethics and monastic purity, when ordained lamas give initiations, they sometimes take off their ordinary robes and wear the clothes of a mahasiddha. When I received a Heruka initiation from one of my gurus, he came dressed like this. There are also photographs of Je Pabongka Rinpoche and His Holiness Trijang Rinpoche wearing mahasiddha clothes. Visualizing all the lineage gurus in mahasiddha aspect is very powerful in breaking down our ordinary concepts. A different manifestation inspires a different vision.

It is the same for us. If we want to engage in tantric practice, we should follow Naropa's example and give up our concern with our appearance and reputation, with the way we look and what people think of us. Perhaps we should take off our clothes and sit on a tiger skin with ashes on our body like an Indian sadhu. When Claudio and another of my Italian students, Piero, first came to see me years ago, they came dressed as mahasiddhas. When they came to the teaching, they even brought an animal skin to sit on.

Different aspects can give us different energy according to our needs. For me, Milarepa is a good example. When I was studying philosophy as a young monk, I often read Milarepa's biography. It made a deep impression on me and took away all difficulties. Another image that inspires me is the fasting Buddha. It is useful sometimes to look at this ascetic aspect of Shakyamuni Buddha. It makes us think, "He was a human being like me. How did he do these things?"

So, Guru Vajradhara is in the space in front of you. Light radiates from his heart into the ten directions, where all the lineage lamas as mahasiddhas sit paying attention to you.

At this point you can perform the seven-limb prayer with a mandala offering, as well as external, internal, secret, and suchness offerings.[2] Offerings do not necessarily have to be material. Giving material offerings, such as money, is easy; the offering of practice is much more difficult. Milarepa said, "I have no worldly offerings to give my guru. I have only the offering of meditation." That is the very best offering. The best offering in the world that you can give your guru is to practice sincerely, be integrated and happy, and achieve realizations.

Next, with strong recognition of Guru Vajradhara as the deity, the daka and dakini, and the Dharma protector, pray strongly to Guru Vajradhara and the lineage lamas for whatever realization you need. They energize and inspire you to develop all the realizations. Because we are practicing the Six Yogas of Naropa, we should make strong prayers for success in inner fire meditation and for quick accomplishment of the inner fire realizations; for successful meditation on the illusory body and for quick realization of the illusory body; and for successful meditation on clear light and realization of clear light. Or if you are feeling anxious, dissatisfied, and in need of blissful kundalini energy, pray for your entire nervous system to become intoxicated with this blissful energy and for you to realize the eternal state of bliss.

After making such strong requests, visualize that all the lineage lamas dissolve into Guru Vajradhara. Rays of white, red, then blue light emanate from the *om, āh,* and *hūm* respectively at the crown, throat, and heart of Guru Vajradhara. Radiant white light enters your crown chakra, radiant red light enters your throat chakra, and radiant blue light enters your heart chakra. Your three main chakras are filled and energized with blissful, radiant light. Imagine that all your negativities of body, speech, and mind are purified and that you receive the vase, wisdom, and secret initiations. Much radiant light again emanates from the three places of the guru, but this time simultaneously. Feel that all the imprints of the negativities of body, speech, and mind are simultaneously purified and that you receive the fourth, the word initiation.

To conclude the guru yoga practice, visualize that Guru Vajradhara comes to the crown of your head and absorbs into you. Even though many things manifest in your life to help you, they have one nuclear source: Guru Vajradhara is the guru, the deity, the daka and dakini, and the Dharma protector. Guru Vajradhara comes down your central channel into your heart chakra. Your body is unified with Guru Vajradhara's body; your speech is unified with Guru Vajradhara's speech; and your mind is unified with Guru

Vajradhara's transcendental, blissful wisdom, which is the dharmakaya experience. You experience totality.

The power of totality, no matter whether we call it God-power or Buddha-power, is not somewhere "up there" or "out there." The power is within each of us. Great compassion is within you; wisdom is within you; God and Buddha are within you. If you have a dualistic concept that you are down here and Guru Vajradhara is somewhere up there, you will never comprehend the unity. Guru yoga is profound; it cannot be expressed in mere words.

You can understand the qualities of Guru Vajradhara only according to your own level of spiritual development. You cannot push and you cannot intellectualize. When you understand that there are many different levels, the practice of guru yoga becomes quite reasonable.

In Buddhism, we say that you can see your own level and perhaps project a little above it. For example, when you reach the advanced level of realization known as the path of accumulation, you will be able to see a little of the next stage, the path of preparation. When you reach the path of preparation, you will be able to project some concept of the path of seeing, because you will already have some experience of emptiness; and so on, all the way to enlightenment.[3]

For example, consider the external, internal, and secret meditations of Lama Tsongkhapa Guru Yoga. First you communicate with the external level of Lama Tsongkhapa's knowledge. Next, at a deeper point, you communicate with the internal level. Then, when you go still deeper, you communicate with the secret level. It is the same with Guru Vajradhara.

You should not feel any separation between you and Guru Vajradhara. You should not think, "The guru is so high and I am so low." Instead you have to unify with Guru Vajradhara, dissolving him into you. You recognize your own mind as the dharmakaya experience of Guru Vajradhara. This blissful wisdom consciousness is the absolute guru, and in order to experience it, you need to practice guru yoga.

The dharmakaya is nonsuperstitious and nonconceptual in nature, but our minds are full of superstition. However, merely imagining the dharmakaya experience summons the inspiration and taste of it, just like imagining cheesecake. Simply thinking of the dharmakaya stimulates the dharmakaya experience and automatically stops superstitious thinking. The main idea of guru yoga is to unify our mind with the utter clarity of Guru Vajradhara's wisdom, which is free from superstition.

We must also learn to recognize the guru in each moment. Even if our most egotistical, miserable, dissatisfied mind is present, instead of expanding this egocentric mind we must recognize its dharmakaya nature, its totality-of-the-guru nature. This direct, organic energy is digested into the great wisdom of unification: "You are the guru, you are the deity, you are the daka and dakini, you are the Dharma protector." This is the teaching of tantra.

This is similar to Christianity, which accepts one God as an embodiment of the principle of totality. The Buddhist tantras describe many deities, dakas and dakinis, and Dharma protectors, but in fact they are all embodiments of the one reality of totality. As we develop in the path to enlightenment, we ourselves become the guru, the deity, the daka and dakini, the Dharma protector. We practice guru yoga in order to discover this unity.

PART THREE

Going Beyond Appearances

9. Transforming Death, Intermediate State, and Rebirth

₡ WHY IT IS NECESSARY TO FIRST PRACTICE EVOLUTIONARY STAGE YOGA

After discussing the preliminary practices, Lama Je Tsongkhapa explains the actual practices that are based on these preliminaries, beginning with meditation on evolutionary stage yoga. Highest Yoga Tantra is divided into two stages: the evolutionary stage and the completion stage. The practices of the Six Yogas of Naropa belong to the completion stage.

In evolutionary stage yoga, which some people prefer to call generation stage yoga, we learn to identify ourselves as a Buddha, a deity, a fully enlightened being (see chapter 10). In intensive meditation, we develop the clear and vivid appearance of ourselves as a deity and the divine pride of actually being the deity. In order to do this, however, we must first practice purifying the ordinary experiences of death, intermediate state, and rebirth. This, the essence of evolutionary stage yoga, is accomplished through meditating on the three pure experiences of the dharmakaya (truth body), sambhogakaya (enjoyment body), and nirmanakaya (emanation body). The experience of death is to be transformed into the dharmakaya, the experience of the intermediate state into the sambhogakaya, and the experience of rebirth into the nirmanakaya.

The evolutionary stage practice of purifying the experiences of death, intermediate state, and rebirth happens at the level of mere imagination, not at the level of actual experience. When we think, "Now is the time of the death experience. The four elements are dissolving," we are simply imagining the death process. However, when we practice completion stage yoga, through the power of concentration we actually experience the process that occurs at death, with absorption of the four elements and all the conceptual minds.

The question might arise, If evolutionary stage practice is only at the level of our imagination, why do we need to engage in it at all? Lama Tsongkhapa explains clearly and completely why it is necessary to actualize the evolutionary stage before engaging in completion stage practices. Some Tibetan lamas have stated that the evolutionary stage practice of actualizing the deity is not necessary and can even become an obstacle to reaching completion stage. Lama Tsongkhapa points out here in the text that misconceptions exist in Tibet that meditation on evolutionary yoga is necessary only for receiving worldly realizations and is therefore unnecessary for the accomplishment of the highest realization.

Lama Tsongkhapa explains that all the lineages coming from Marpa[1] say that the first step is to lead students through evolutionary yoga. To demonstrate this point, he quotes a passage from Milarepa, "First you have to go through evolutionary yoga in order to cut the difficult visions of dying, intermediate state, and rebirth." Many other great lamas of the past have agreed that the evolutionary stage has to be actualized as well as the completion stage.

Expressing his own opinion, Lama Tsongkhapa states that the proper basis for success in completion stage yoga is evolutionary stage yoga and that, as a preliminary to completion stage practice, practitioners should have stable concentration on themselves as the deity.

Also, in general, the practice of evolutionary stage yoga should have three qualities, or flavors: all beings should be seen as deities, every experience should be inseparable from the wisdom of nonduality, and every experience should have the nature of great bliss.

Accomplishment of evolutionary yoga is a high realization, with both gross and subtle levels. With the gross level of attainment, you are able to build up a clear mental image of the entire mandala with its various deities, celestial mansion, and surrounding environment. With the subtle level of attainment, you have indestructible samadhi and can vividly imagine your entire mandala, in miniature, for several hours.

However, even though we have not yet achieved the subtle attainment of the evolutionary stage, we can still start completion stage practices such as the Six Yogas of Naropa. You shouldn't feel that inner fire is a big leap. "I'd better meditate on renunciation for the rest of my life. That is more reasonable." Don't think this way! Lama Tsongkhapa, as well as many lamas of other traditions, developed the skill to practice both evolutionary and completion stages in each day. Lama Tsongkhapa's biography explains that in some sessions he practiced evolutionary stage yoga and in others, completion stage. Training in this way helps to bring realizations. It is right to engage in evolutionary and completion stage yogas at the same time because they support each other. For example, sometimes you may find evolutionary stage yoga difficult, but for some reason the completion stage practices seem easier and more familiar, and touch your heart more. When you practice both stages together, you taste the blissful chocolate.

❧ Bringing the three kayas into the path

Lama Tsongkhapa strongly emphasizes that whenever we actualize a deity as the path to liberation, we must use the technique of transforming death, intermediate state, and rebirth into the three kayas and bringing the three kayas into the path to enlightenment. This is the essential practice of evolutionary stage, and it fruitfully and suitably leads to the completion stage.

How do we engage in evolutionary stage practice? Generally, regardless of which deity we are actualizing, evolutionary stage yoga involves the practice of a daily *sadhana*. The sadhana begins with taking refuge and generating a bodhicitta motivation to achieve enlightenment in order to benefit others. This is followed by the practice of guru yoga, the root of the entire tantric path, as I described earlier.

After this, just before meditating on the three kayas, we recite the emptiness mantra *oṃ svabhāvaśuddhāḥ sarvadharmāḥ svabhāvaśuddho 'ham* and meditate on its profound meaning. Basically, this mantra states that the nature of everything that exists is pure, that all existent phenomena, including us, are nondual in character. It is referring to the non-self-existence, the noninherent existence, or the emptiness of everything that exists. This is absolute reality. Conventional reality is like a dream, a magician's trick, a projection, or a mirage. Thinking in this way as we recite the emptiness mantra dissolves our concrete concepts.

Our normal dualistic mind constantly distorts reality. We either add extra qualities to reality or we underestimate it. We never seem to find the middle way. We project impurity upon the pure. "I was born with impurities, I am impure now, I will die impure and end up in hell." Even if we don't consciously think this, it is there inside us. We believe we are fundamentally impure. "How can I be pure?" our self-pity mind thinks. We must rid ourselves of this idea, which is the cause of all our diseases of body and mind.

The point is that the fundamental nature of our mind is pure and spacelike. Ego-mind tries to project something impure on top of this, but it is impossible to add to something that is spacelike in nature. Such impure projections are momentary, like clouds in the sky. Even though the sky allows the coming and going of clouds, they are not a permanent characteristic of the sky. A similar relationship exists between the fundamental character of our mind and our dualistic mind. The nonduality nature of our mind has always been pure, is pure now, and will always be pure. What we call "impurities" are the superficial clouds of ego that come and go. We have to recognize that they are transitory and that they can be removed. They are simply energy. Their relative, negative, confused, fantasy nature is not our fundamental nature. Realizing this cuts off the self-pity ego.

The whole point of doing meditation is to discover this fundamental principle of totality. The moment you reach this experience of nonduality you have no room for heavy emotions or sentimentality. The pure, penetrative awareness cuts through relative obstacles and touches the deepest nature of human existence. At that moment of experience there is no conceptual labeling by the dualistic mind; at that moment, there is no Buddha or God, no subject or object, no heaven or hell.

After reciting *oṃ svabhāvaśuddhāḥ sarvadharmāḥ svabhāvaśuddho 'ham,* you visualize the process that occurs at death, starting with the dissolution of the four elements. Feel the absorption of the earth element, then the water element. Your experience of the sensory world gradually diminishes. The fire element absorbs, then the air element. All your concrete concepts gradually dissolve too.

Now you experience only consciousness; your body has ceased to function. The white vision appears; you see the entire universe as empty space pervaded by white light. No dualistic phenomena appear. You are approaching the universal totality of nonduality, your true nature. Feel, "I am this natural state of consciousness touching universal reality."

Your mind becomes more subtle, and the white vision changes into the red vision. Maintain mindfulness and simply let go. Experience the unified nature of the emptiness and bliss of the red vision.

Now you experience the black vision, like the early morning before sunrise. Out of the darkness comes light, signaling the beginning of the clear light experience. Like the sun rising in a clear sky, the light grows and grows, until the entire space appears as clear light. This is the dharmakaya experience, the most subtle consciousness. All existence is nondual. All the dualistic puzzles have disappeared. You enter the spacelike nature of clear light. Your wisdom consciousness embraces universal space.

You don't need to analyze the nature of the non-self-existent I; simply experiencing the nonexistence of the self as spacelike is good enough. Know that this space is not your usual self-pity ego-image. It is a clean-clear, natural state with no complicated ego conflicts or relativity puzzles. This is the real experience. Rest in it.

Intellectualizing about emptiness can sometimes become an obstacle to discovering emptiness. An intellectual would say, "Wait a minute, Lama Yeshe. You say that emptiness is like empty space, but this is too easy. This is not Nagarjuna's philosophical view of emptiness." You could argue that what I have said has no connotation of the Prasangika-Madhyamakan view of emptiness, or even of the Chittamatrin view. You could argue with me on the point for a whole lifetime, but it would be a rubbish argument; you could write a big book about it, but it would be a complete waste of time.

When we study philosophy, we have to know each point precisely, but when we are practicing, we just have to act. We have to begin the experience of emptiness somewhere, and space is the prime example used by all Tibetan lamas to represent nonduality. The main point is that we are trying to have an experience that goes beyond mundane ego puzzles.

From the philosophical point of view, emptiness has no form, no color, no smell, and so forth, and we can understand this from our own experiences of emptiness. In the moment of experience, the sensory world has no way to magnetize your mind. The narrow, dualistic puzzles disappear, allowing the natural state of mind to radiate and embrace reality.

Here we want our consciousness to experience the clear light without conceptualization; it's like rays of sunlight embracing the blue sky of morning. This clear light is the great universal emptiness of nonduality. Experience only the total unity of the dharmakaya. Feel, "I am this enlightened dharmakaya state, this total peace and joy, this unified intense awareness." See all appearances as reflections of this dharmakaya consciousness. Stay as long as you can in this experience of omnipresent wisdom, this state of nonduality.

Every tantric practice is related to something natural within our normal experience. Here, the experience of clear light is similar to the experience at the time of death, when all the gross consciousnesses, both sensory and conceptual, have naturally ceased to function. After these minds have dissolved, you experience the natural state of the clear light of death.

In the very subtle state of the dharmakaya you can communicate only with other enlightened beings. Therefore, in order to communicate with sentient beings and benefit them, you must move from the dharmakaya to the sambhogakaya and then to the nirmanakaya. How do you do this?

Some texts say that at this point you should recall the bodhicitta motivation you generated at the beginning of the meditation and think, "As long as I remain in the dharmakaya experience, nobody can see me. Therefore, in order to benefit others, I must manifest in the sambhogakaya." This sounds a little awkward to me. If you have already motivated at the beginning, why should you start this kind of conversation with yourself again while you are meditating on emptiness? Why bring in some dualistic puzzle and distract yourself? My advice is that you should motivate at the beginning and then just float through the rest of the meditation.

You will know from your own experience when you are ready to move from the dharmakaya to the sambhogakaya. At that time visualize that a blue *nada* appears from the space of nonduality. Or, if it is easier for you, visualize a shaft of blue light, a candle flame, or the syllable *hūṃ*. It is not necessary to do this exactly as I say or exactly as described in the texts. Be flexible in your practice; tailor the meditation to suit your own experience. The point is that the sambhogakaya has to have some relationship to the intermediate state, which is subtle, so your sambhogakaya experience should also be subtle.

The nada, representing your consciousness, manifests like a subtle, blue cloud in space. Unify with this blissful blue light. Feel that this is you, your sambhogakaya, your illusory body, your psychic body, your rainbow body. Simultaneously you experience nonduality and the divine pride of being the sambhogakaya. Meditate on this experience.

Because only higher bodhisattvas can communicate with the sambhogakaya and lesser beings cannot do so, you eventually shift to the nirmanakaya so that all beings can communicate with you.

You look down from the space of nonduality and see the blissful energy of a radiant white light with a reddish hue. This is a moon, and your consciousness, the blue light, lands in the center of it. The moon is very bright, radiant, and blissful in nature, and it represents the totally developed, blissful male and female kundalini energy of the Buddhas. The texts mention that this is similar to when, from the intermediate state after death, your consciousness enters the drop formed by your father's sperm and your mother's ovum. But here, instead of feeling attraction to the father's or mother's liquid energy, as you do when you are in the actual intermediate state, you see the energy as father Heruka and mother Vajravarahi. You land in this incredibly blissful kundalini energy. This male and female sexual energy then radiates and embraces all universal energy.

At the center of the moon disk, your psyche transforms into the radiant, blue light-body of Heruka, embracing your consort Vajravarahi, who is red in color. Your entire nervous system is filled with bliss. You experience no concepts, no fantasy projections, no emotional disturbances. Vajravarahi represents the universal totality of female energy and Heruka represents the universal totality of male energy. Their embracing signifies the union of the entire fundamental universal reality.

A reflection of your dharmakaya nature is transmitted through the sambhogakaya to the nirmanakaya form of Heruka. Your form is a rainbow light-body, a crystal body, a psychic body, an illusory body. You experience great bliss and great wisdom of nonduality. With strong divine pride, think, "I am Heruka. I am the unity of this energy of great bliss and great wisdom."

The clear and vivid appearance of yourself as the deity and your divine pride of actually being the deity eliminate the concrete concepts of your self-pitying imagination. There is no room for them. Feel this, and let go.

10. Arising as a Divine Being

To succeed in tantric practice it is essential to identify yourself strongly as a deity. You need to have intense awareness of your body as the deity's body, your speech as the deity's mantra, and your mind as great blissful wisdom.

The purpose of seeing yourself as a deity and the environment as the deity's mandala is to transcend mundane appearances and actions. The deity and the mandala are manifestations of simultaneously born blissful wisdom. There are different traditions concerning the deity to visualize when you practice the Six Yogas of Naropa. Some lamas use Hevajra, some Vajrayogini, and others Heruka. There are also different traditions of Heruka, such as the lineages of Luhipa and Drilbupa. The deity you use, however, should belong to Highest Yoga Tantra; Action Tantra deities, for example, are not suitable. In fact, you can manifest as any deity you wish: Vajradhara, Vajrasattva, Vajrayogini, Guhyasamaja, or Yamantaka.[1]

Why are there so many different deities in tantra? Because each deity arouses different feelings and activates different qualities within us. Choose for your practice whichever deity feels most familiar to you. Many lineage lamas have used Heruka; in my opinion he is the most powerful deity in this twentieth century, so I am describing the practices in relation to visualizing yourself as Heruka.

No matter which deity you choose to visualize, Lama Tsongkhapa recommends that at the time of practicing the completion stage, instead of emanating the entire mandala, you visualize yourself in the simple form of the deity and consort, which means with one face and two arms. And even though in general you should visualize the elaborate form of the deity during evolutionary stage practice, if you find so much detail distracting, just visualize yourself in the simple form of the deity. This is sufficient in the beginning.

You have arisen from the sambhogakaya as the nirmanakaya form of Heruka, with a body of radiant blue light. You are standing, have four faces and twelve arms, and are embracing Vajravarahi, who has a body of radiant red light. You need to have a clear and vivid appearance of yourself as the deity, visualizing every detail as precisely as you can.

When you begin your meditation session, focus your attention at the top of the deity's body and slowly move downward, contemplating one area at a time. Then move from the bottom to the top. Once you are familiar with the visualization, hold in your mind the complete image of the deity, focusing neither too tightly nor too loosely. Eventually your visualization will be perfect. Also, remember to energize bliss and nonduality.

Don't worry if you find it difficult to see yourself as Heruka in the way he is depicted in Tibetan paintings. Your body is already beautiful and handsome, so leave it as it is and simply change its color. Actually, seeing yourself as a deity has nothing to do with Tibetan culture. You think you are not involved with a culture when you project your usual self-pity image of yourself, but in fact you are. Instead of seeing yourself in that way, transform yourself into blissful, radiant, blue light and cultivate strong divine pride.

The special characteristics of Heruka are universal love and compassion. We all need love and compassion, don't we? We are craving for someone to love us and take care of us. Heruka manifests our archetypal ideal so that we can identify ourselves with the energy of universal love and compassion and actually become universal love and compassion. Our worries about whether or not someone loves us disappear when we generate the strength of love, compassion, and wisdom.

You can see how this works in your everyday life. No one wants to come near you when you are full of self-pity or having a nervous breakdown. People feel uncomfortable around you. But when you are full of love and compassion, you can't keep people away from you. This is natural. Because we are looking for happiness, we don't want to go near miserable people.

Heruka's face is handsome but slightly wrathful, laughing but also frowning slightly. Why is universal love and compassion depicted in this way? Because this is what we need. When we receive even a little bit of love, we become emotional and out of control. That's not good, because the other person can't handle you when you are like that. There needs to be a middle way.

Tantra teaches us that we need powerful transformation. Identifying with the profound qualities of Heruka and seeing ourselves as infinite, radiant, blue light are powerful methods for eliminating self-pity concepts and garbage-imagination.

What is our main problem? It is that we think, "I am the worst person in the world. I am full of hatred, desire, and ignorance." These concepts are totally negative, and you must purify them. From the time you were born until now, you have been carrying around this self-pity view. Cry, cry, fear, fear, emotion, emotion. Obsessed with your own shortcomings, you put tremendous pressure on yourself. You punish yourself by regarding yourself as ugly and worthless. Other people may think you are beautiful, but still you project yourself as ugly.

Tantra says that essentially every human being is divine and pure. This is why it is important to identify yourself so strongly as being a deity, to regard yourself as perfectly developed. Instead of seeing your body as something miserable, transform it into a radiant blue light-body. Outwardly this might seem strange, but inwardly there is a profound meaning. Blue light symbolizes nonduality, so the moment you visualize this blue light, which is like clear blue sky, your dualistic, concrete concepts break down; you no longer believe in them.

This is not a philosophical point or a matter of blind faith—you can experience it. From the tantric point of view, each color we perceive—blue, red, yellow, or whatever—is directly related to what is happening in our internal world. It is important to be aware of this.

The radiant blue light of Heruka helps us to touch reality, which is the most important thing in the world. The Heruka mandala expresses inner and outer reality rather than a fantasy world of projections. Most of us are unaware of reality; we never touch it.

Western actors explain that when they play a particular role in a movie, they have to go through some of the experiences of that person in order to express his feelings and actions realistically. Because of his training, the actor somehow carries deep inside himself the person he is portraying, even when he is not acting. It is the same when you become Heruka. Your psychic energy has to transform convincingly into the blissful, radiant blue light-body of Heruka.

Westerners often have a problem with deities. They think, "Why should I see myself as Heruka? This is just another fantasy, another delusion. It is difficult enough for me just to be a man or a woman. I have enough trouble in this world with my complicated views of who I am and of how to relate to a man's world or a woman's world. Now I have to change my appearance and wear another mask—a Heruka mask."

Actually, you do not visualize yourself as Heruka in order to show a different manifestation; Heruka is the manifestation of the profound qualities you already have within you. Heruka is within you. To ask why you need to manifest as Heruka means that you don't understand that the quality of the deity is the quality of your own being. To recognize and comprehend your profound qualities, you visualize yourself as Heruka rather than identifying with your usual feelings of being ugly and unwanted. Tantra considers it very important to eradicate such symptoms of ego. There is no point in holding garbage-concepts of yourself. You are perfect; you just need to recognize it. According to tantra, you do not need to wait until your next life to experience heaven. Heaven is now. Tantra teaches us to bring heaven into our everyday life. Our home is heaven, and everyone we see is a god or goddess.

You are not your face, your blood, your bones, or any other part of your body. The essence of you and your life is your consciousness, your mind, your psyche. Your body is basically a robot being pushed around by a computer; it is the manifestation of the computer of your consciousness.

From the time you were born until now, you have manifested in many different ways. Sometimes you were angry and looked like a monster and at other times you were peaceful and beautiful. These manifestations of anger, jealousy, loving kindness, great compassion, or great wisdom do not come from your blood and bones but from the power of your consciousness. We think that the body is the boss. Overwhelmed and intoxicated by the pleasures of our body, we disregard the mind, and it ends up as the slave of our body. However, it is our mind that puts us in a miserable concentration camp, not our body.

The point is that the mind is powerful and can manifest anything. When you can convincingly see yourself as beautiful and handsome, your self-pity concepts will vanish and you will become the manifestation of your own profound qualities. Everyone can achieve this.

Actually, we have more than one body, as we will discuss soon (see chapter 11). As well as our physical body, we have a more subtle psychic body. Our consciousness does have the ability to manifest as a radiant blue light-body, and when we understand the nature of the subtle body, we can learn to manipulate the energy of our inner nervous system and to control our blood-and-bone body.

When you visualize yourself as Heruka in union with Vajravarahi, it is important to feel that you actually are the deity, that you are youthful, beautiful, fully developed sexually, and full of kundalini. Some people think that we only pretend to be Heruka. This is not right. We are not pretending. The more strongly you identify yourself as the deity, the more transformation you achieve and the more fear and uncontrolled emotion you eliminate.

We often say that we don't like to waste time, but we do waste time when we participate in self-pity and the fearful "I." Kick out self-pity by generating the strong divine pride of being the pure deity. Do not merely pretend to be the deity. Have the inner conviction that you are the deity. If you feel unified with Heruka, transformation will naturally occur. Even when you are not in a formal meditation session, you may be surprised to find that you are still Heruka.

And remember that all appearances are illusory and nondual in nature and that all the illusions are empty. Recognize also that all the empty illusions are blissful in nature. Focus your attention on this blissful state.

When we receive the Heruka Body-Mandala initiation, we are usually required to recite and meditate on the long sadhana as a daily commitment. However, when we are practicing inner fire meditation in an intensive retreat, we can cut down on words and prayers. This means that in order to arise as Heruka, we can use the short sadhana *The Yoga of the Three Purifications*, which contains both the Vajrasattva and Heruka meditations.

I have not made up this shortcut approach. His Holiness Trijang Rinpoche, an actual manifestation of Heruka, mentioned this during his teachings on the Six Yogas. The point is that when you are actualizing completion stage yoga, because you are spending most of your time in intensive meditation, you don't need many words. This makes sense. Reading too many prayers can cause you to lose the real taste of the practice.

Taking a shortcut like this out of laziness is not acceptable; but if you are meditating intensively on completion stage, you have no time to read pieces of paper. Sometimes people are so caught up in details that they lose the overall picture. For example, if you have to recite twenty-four sadhanas every day and each sadhana takes you an hour to recite, what is the result? You cannot practice the Six Yogas of Naropa in this way. When you read your sadhanas, you have to look at the pieces of paper; but when you practice inner fire, you just have to close your eyes.

I also think that it is not necessary to read all the words of a sadhana if you perform all the meditations. If you remember the process from beginning to end and have a complete mental picture of all the meditations, you do not need to read the words. Once you have performed the meditations, what is there left to do? Words can definitely be an obstacle.

However, even if we use a shortcut method, we still need to make the meditation rich. Therefore, although the process of meditating on the three kayas is not actually described in *The Yoga of the Three Purifications*, you should include it. As Lama Tsongkhapa explains, this meditation makes the practice profound.

The meditation on the three kayas does not have to be complicated. Simply bring the experience of the highest realizations of the states of dharmakaya, sambhogakaya, and nirmanakaya into the present time. Don't think, "This practice is too high for me." Simply imagine the experience and bring it into the present moment. Meditating on the three kayas is a necessary preparation for the completion stage practices. If you want to make a good chocolate cake, you have to make good preparations.

〰

I want you to understand the teachings and to be technically clear about the meditations. Then I want you to practice. Many of my students have been working with evolutionary stage yoga for several years now, but the evolutionary stage is a little like dreaming. With completion stage yoga, however, you are in the real situation and are no longer dreaming. Be careful, because if you push the wrong button, you are going to end up in the wrong place.

Everybody should try these meditations. If you never try, you can never be successful; but if you try, you might surprise yourself. Anyone practicing the Six Yogas of Naropa should expect to work hard. These meditations are not meant to be written down on pieces of paper and intellectualized. It is important to hear the teachings, but after hearing them, you must meditate and gain experiences. I have no interest in the Six Yogas of Naropa as an intellectual exercise.

I want you to be inspired by these teachings. What we are doing is something serious, and I want you to be serious. So please practice. It is very simple; it is not complicated. Milarepa and many other yogis like him had much renunciation and put much effort into this practice. For many years they lived in mountain caves like animals, eating nettles and grass. Remember the tremendous effort Naropa put into pursuing these teachings. He almost died twelve times. On the other hand, we live in such comfortable situations. It would be shameful not to put any effort into meditating. Milarepa was the right extreme; we lean toward the wrong extreme.

The Six Yogas of Naropa is a very profound teaching, so we should use it in a meaningful way. It is so worthwhile. I want everyone to taste some satisfaction, to have a profound experience. I want you really to touch something deep inside yourself, then you will definitely experience some transformation.

If you don't have any experiences now, during the course, I am almost certain that you won't have any later—when you go home you will go back to your old habits. But if you meditate strongly now you will really taste the practice, and then you will be inspired to continue your meditations.

If we are successful here, I would like to teach the Six Yogas again and again. I cannot help but teach it again. When I started teaching Western people, I saw that you responded well. Whether you are capable or not, you try to meditate. I have seen that the Buddha-dharma helped Western people: that's why I became interested in you. I got so much energy to teach you. I pray that I can teach you the Six Yogas of Naropa again.

11. The Characteristics of Body and Mind

We come now to the actual teaching on the completion stage yogas. Lama Je Tsongkhapa begins by describing the basis of these yogas, the body and the mind. He first explains the characteristics of mind and then those of body, but other commentaries often explain the characteristics of the body first. Although there is no significant difference, Western people might find the second approach easier. Therefore, I will first explain the nature of the body and then that of the mind.

❧ CHARACTERISTICS OF THE BODY

Lama Tsongkhapa actually explains the characteristics of the body in a way different from other commentaries, and we can cover this later (see chapter 15, p. 117). I will now explain them according to the other commentaries.

The body can be said to exist simultaneously on three levels. These are the gross body, the subtle body, and the very subtle body. The gross body is composed of the blood, bones, five sense organs, and so forth.

The subtle body, also known as the vajra body, comprises the channels and the energy-winds and drops that exist within the channels. There are thousands of these subtle physical channels running throughout our body. The main ones that we use in meditation are the central channel, which runs up and down our body just in front of the spine, and the two side channels, which run alongside the central channel. At various points along the central channel, smaller channels branch off to form channel wheels, or *chakras*. I will discuss the channels and chakras in more detail later (see chapter 14).

The energy-winds, or airs, that we are discussing do not refer to the air that we breathe in from the outside world, but to the subtle winds that flow throughout our channels. These subtle winds enable our bodies to function and are associated with different levels of mind.[1] In tantra there is a saying, "The mind rides on the wind." This means that our consciousness is mounted on the winds; they always move together through the subtle channels. We are working with and learning to control these winds during inner fire meditation.

Our vajra body also contains subtle liquid energy, the red and white drops. The Tibetan word for these drops is *tigle*, but I prefer to use the Hindu term *kundalini* because it is more universal. The tantras also refer to the drops as *bodhicitta*. Actually, in Tibetan we say *kun-da da-bu jang-sem*, which translates as "moon-like bodhicitta." Although these red and white drops are always together in all the channels, the female red drops predominate at the navel chakra and the male white drops at the crown chakra. (Some tantric practices speak of the kundalini drops as deities; they say that dakas and dakinis dance throughout the nervous system.)

The third aspect of the body, the very subtle body, manifests at the time of death. After the absorptions of the four elements comes the experience of the three visions: the white, red, and black visions. After these, the clear light of death arises. The subtle states of consciousness that experience these visions, referred to as "the four empties," are simultaneously accompanied by subtle wind energy, the most subtle being the wind that accompanies the clear light mind in the indestructible drop at the heart chakra. This subtlest of winds is the very subtle body.

When the yogi or yogini arises from the experience of clear light wisdom, this very subtle wind manifests as an illusory body. With achievement of the illusory body, a very high attainment, there is total unity of body and mind. At present we don't have good communication between body and mind. Our bodies and minds have different energies and are not unified with each other.

Understanding the subtle body and the very subtle body helps us to recognize that we have other bodies within us in addition to our physical body—so we don't have to worry too much when our gross body is degenerating or being uncooperative.

The tantric teachings also explain the germination and evolution of human beings: how the consciousness in the intermediate state perceives the male and female energy of the parents and is attracted to it, then enters the fertilized egg. As I described earlier (see chapter 9), in tantric meditation you visualize the male and female energy as a white moon with a reddish hue and yourself as radiant light that lands in the center of it. This corresponds to your own rebirth.

Western explanations of how the egg and sperm enter the mother's womb and of the subsequent development of the fetus are very similar to those in the tantric teachings. I was amazed at the similarities when I saw a television documentary about this process. Tibetans have the words but not the visual presentation; Westerners put it all on film. Sometimes I don't know what is going on in your minds culturally, so I hesitate to tell you certain Buddhist ideas. Seeing this film, however, encouraged me. Tibetans explain how the fetus develops, with the wind energies pushing this way and that; how the heart chakra is the first chakra to develop; how the channels grow from there; and then how the other channels develop. We have detailed explanations of how energy develops and functions to coordinate the internal and external.

Also, the Kalachakra Tantra gives very interesting explanations about the relationship between the sun, moon, stars, and time, and between internal energy and the external universe, as well as advice on how to meditate on these things. We have incredibly detailed information about all of these subjects.[2]

It is important to learn these kinds of scientific details, and this is illustrated by the following story. Vasubandhu and his brother Asanga once had a competition to see who could best describe a calf that was still in its mother's womb. Asanga investigated telepathically and saw that the calf had a white patch on its forehead. Vasubandhu, however, understood how the body of a calf actually lies in a cow's womb; he realized that his brother had made a mistake because he could not integrate the information he had received telepathically. He said, "The forehead is not white. The tip of the tail is white." Vasubandhu understood that the tail of the calf had curled all the way forward to the forehead and that the white spot on the forehead Asanga saw telepathically was in fact the tip of the calf's tail. When the calf was born, it was seen that Vasubandhu's scientific understanding had won over Asanga's telepathic power.

It is very useful to understand the nature of the vajra body and how it functions, because you can then learn to manipulate its different energies. You can learn how to approach the pleasure centers and misery centers and how to switch them on and off. For example, if you are familiar with your entire nervous system, you can alleviate any pain you experience. To release tension in your upper body you might have to massage a point in your lower body. By knowing the interrelationships within your body, you can relieve the discomfort. According to tantra, pain in a particular area of the body is often due to energy blockages, which in turn are related to blocked states of mind. If you understand the fundamental structure of your body, you will know how to release any tension that arises.

Your body is organic, and you need to learn to listen to its rhythms until you feel that each cell in your nervous system is talking to you. When you develop such sensitive awareness of your body, it is almost as though you can tell it what to do. Instead of clomping around heavily, your whole body feels light and blissful, as if you are walking on air. It is liberating. Simply touching yourself will produce bliss. We have that resource. Instead of being a source of pain, your entire body can become a source of bliss. You reach a point where your body and mind cooperate so perfectly that you feel body is mind and mind is body. There is an incredible sense of unity.

We pay a lot of attention to our body. However, we concentrate our efforts merely on externals, such as cleanliness and appearance. In the Six Yogas of Naropa we are dealing instead with the subtle body, the vajra body. By utilizing various meditation techniques, we learn to control the energies of this vajra body, especially the wind energy; and because the mind rides on the wind, we are able to direct the mind wherever we want. Eventually we can direct it to enlightenment. This is why it is important to educate ourselves about the nature of our subtle nervous system.

◆ CHARACTERISTICS OF THE MIND

The mind also has three divisions: the gross mind, the subtle mind, and the very subtle mind. The gross mind is composed of the five sense perceptions, which are very limited, crude judges of phenomena. The subtle mind includes the six root delusions, the twenty branch delusions—in fact, all the eighty conceptual minds.[3] These minds are subtle in the sense that it is difficult to understand their characteristics and functions. It is difficult for us to understand how they hold concepts and how they bring the various problems of life.

Let's take the example of desire, one of the six root delusions. We do not really understand what desire means. In the West, desire seems to refer to sense gratification. However, in the Buddhist view, desire is not a craving of the senses but the mental concepts and projections that we build up on an object, thereby bringing us problems. Desire misinterprets and distorts the object; we then hallucinate and drive ourselves crazy.

I am always skeptical when somebody says that they know the meaning of desire. It is not easy to understand desire. I think it is very difficult, and it takes time. If you know the nature of desire, you can really control your mind because you are able to question and to understand your own view of desire's objects. Otherwise, you cannot see the mind's tricks. With its constant "I feel, I want," desire plays tricks on you, leading you to a constant restlessness that can mess up your life. Desire makes countries confused: the East and the West are confused because of desire; the Middle East is confused because of desire. Husband and wife are confused because of desire. Even disciple and teacher can be confused because of desire.

Don't arrogantly think that you know everything about desire. To really understand desire, you have to put much time and effort into investigating it with strong meditation. With meditation, you can definitely understand desire; without meditation, you cannot. You can listen to explanations about desire for a year, but you will still only understand it intellectually. To comprehend desire you have to go inside yourself and build a solid understanding there. It is not enough to have some dull, vague understanding.

The third aspect of the mind is the very subtle mind. This is the clear light mind, which is inseparable from the very subtle wind in the indestructible drop at the heart.[4] Everybody experiences this very subtle mind when they die.

The subtle body and subtle mind are not possessed by only a few special people. We all have them. We learn to activate these subtle levels of our body and mind in the completion stage practice of inner fire, and we then use them to achieve enlightenment.

12. Unifying Relative and Absolute

Some texts on the Six Yogas of Naropa describe various characteristics of the gross, subtle, and very subtle minds, and I have also described them briefly. In *Having the Three Convictions*, however, Lama Tsongkhapa emphasizes that the fundamental point is to understand the absolute nature of the mind, which is emptiness. He therefore goes into this topic in great detail.

Lama Tsongkhapa begins by quoting from *The Hevajra Tantra in Two Sections*, which says that there is no mind that perceives form, sound, smell, taste, or touch. Lama Tsongkhapa interprets this to mean that the mind does not have an innate, self-existent character. However, the mind does exist relatively as an interdependent phenomenon.

Lama Tsongkhapa says that non-self-existence is the original character of all phenomena, including the mind. He points out that it is not that phenomena are first self-existent and then become non-self-existent by means of logical reasoning. This is not the case, although it almost seems as if it is. Non-self-existence is not simply some philosophical idea but Lord Buddha's scientific explanation of the nature of all phenomena.

The mind is essentially pure and free from duality. Some schools of thought regard unimportant phenomena as non-self-existent, whereas they see important phenomena such as the mind as absolute and therefore self-existent. However, in Nagarjuna's view, there are no exceptions; all phenomena are non-self-existent. Buddha has the same lack of self-existence as a garbage bag. There is no such thing as a self-existent, or dualistically existent, Buddha. The totality of a garbage bag, the totality of Buddha, and our totality are one.

According to the Buddhist point of view, mind is the creator of the world. It creates everything, including our happiness and our problems. Yet even the potential of the mind to create phenomena does not have a self-existent character. This potential exists because of the nondual nature of the mind, because of the unity of the mind's absolute, non-self-existent nature and its relative, interdependent nature. This nature is not something that we have to invent; it is already there. We just have to realize it.

In *Having the Three Convictions* Lama Tsongkhapa also quotes one of Marpa's songs, in which Marpa describes how he traveled east near the Ganges River, where he met his guru Je Maitripa. Through Maitripa's great kindness, Marpa discovered the fundamental "nongrowing" nature. This refers to non-self-existence, or emptiness. Marpa continues, "I beheld the face of the clear light of the subtle consciousness, saw the three kayas, and cut through all relative, conventional puzzles."

Lama Tsongkhapa then quotes Je Maitripa, who says in *Ten Reflections on Simple Suchness* that anyone who wishes to find the proper understanding of reality, of emptiness, should not follow the philosophical doctrines of the Vaibashika, Sautrantika, Chittamatra, or Svatantrika-Madhyamaka schools. The teaching on emptiness to follow is that of the Prasangika-Madhyamaka, as expounded by Nagarjuna and Chandrakirti. Compared to their interpretation of emptiness, all other views seem second-rate.

An understanding of Nagarjuna's experience is especially important for success in completion stage yogas such as the Six Yogas of Naropa. Of course, a proper understanding of the Chittamatrin and Svatantrika-Madhyamakan interpretation will take you part of the way.

The main point to understand is that in an absolute sense the mind is empty, or non-self-existent, while relatively it exists in dependence upon causes and conditions and so forth. All the phenomena of samsara and nirvana, including the mind, exist like an illusion, a dream, or a reflection in a mirror.

Even though it is sometimes said that something is nonexistent because it is like an illusion, a dream, or a reflection in a mirror, this is not philosophically correct. It is speaking loosely to say, "This phenomenon does not exist because it is an illusion. It is just one of my projections." In fact, the reverse is true. The phenomenon exists precisely because it exists as an illusion, which is interdependent. A reflection in a mirror is also interdependent; it exists because of the mirror.

Also, you cannot say that the mind and the objects of the illusory world are nonexistent in the way that the horn on a rabbit's head is nonexistent. The rabbit's horn does not exist even relatively, but the mind does. Lama Tsongkhapa is saying, "Wait a minute. Stop! You are going too far." There is a danger that we won't understand the unity of relative and absolute existence.

Our problem is that we are too extreme. Take a tissue, for example. The minute we say that the tissue exists, a self-existent projection comes to our minds. When we then talk about the nonduality of the tissue, the tissue seems to disappear, and we have the impression that the tissue cannot even function as a tissue. This is not the way it is. In the space of nonduality the tissue is made, bought, and used. The tissue *is* nonduality.

We think that the tissue is functioning in a concrete, self-existent way, but Lama Tsongkhapa does not agree at all. It has a subjective origin and an objective, non-self-existent character within it; therefore, it functions. Nor can you say that non-self-existence is here in this space and you then put the tissue into it. Non-self-existence is unified with this tissue. Nonduality totally embraces every part of this tissue.

When we describe the nonduality, the non-self-existence, of the tissue, it is not that the tissue is first self-existent and that we then push philosophically to make it non-self-existent. There is no way to push. Lama Tsongkhapa is going to say that because the tissue exists in its own particular way, it has the characteristic of nonduality.

Every activity, from coming together to breaking apart, happens because of the universal reality of nonduality. It is the same with every movement of energy—growing, interacting, transforming. Within the movement of energy, there is no self-existent motion. Part of my nature is this tissue's nature; part of your nature is tissue-paper nature. You probably don't want to have tissue-paper nature, but in an absolute sense, there is no difference between a tissue's nature and your nature.

Sometimes we push too much when we apply logic in order to understand emptiness—"This is non-self-existent because of this and that reason." By simply looking at a situation, however, we can see that the situation itself expresses nonduality. This is why Lama Tsongkhapa says that dependent-arising is the king of logic: "This tissue is non-self-existent because it is a dependent-arising."

Nonduality does not mean nonexistence. A tissue exists relatively because it functions. You can touch it, use it to wipe your nose, and then throw it away. It comes and goes. In that sense it exists conventionally, but it does not have the solid existence that it superficially appears to have. Even though it appears to exist dualistically, it does not have a dualistic way of existing.

To say that something exists simply means that it functions, that conventionally it does something. That is all. It is momentary and it functions. But when we talk about absolute nature, we are speaking about a broader view, a bigger view. The absolute nature of a thing is part of you, part of me, part of mozzarella cheese, part of chocolate.

Existence is for the relative mind only. Even good and bad exist in dependence on the mind, the time, the situation, the environment, and so forth. For example, perhaps at one time it was considered good to give a potato as a gift, but nowadays a person who received such a gift would be shocked. Good and bad are relative. But at the same time there is a broader reality within the space of a thing. When you experience the totality, the nonduality, of a phenomenon, it is like space.

Here in *Having the Three Convictions* Lama Tsongkhapa quotes Milarepa: "The omnipresent Lord Buddha explained that all phenomena exist only for those of unintelligent mind." What does he mean by "unintelligent"? Milarepa is referring to the narrow, relative mind. According to the absolute view, there is no Buddha, no subject of meditation, and no meditator; there is no path, no wisdom, and no nirvana. There is nothing. All these are merely labels, names, words.

This means that there is no *self-existent* samsara or nirvana. Milarepa points out that, relatively, if there were no suffering sentient beings, there would be no past, present, or future Buddhas. There would also be no karma; and if there were no cause and effect, how could there be samsara or nirvana? Milarepa's point is that all samsara-phenomena and nirvana-phenomena exist only for the conventional, relative mind. Lama Tsongkhapa agrees that Milarepa's interpretation of relative and absolute is perfectly correct.

Lama Tsongkhapa has a wonderful way of putting things together. In this text he describes the characteristics of mind, both relative and absolute, in an unusual and profound way. The way he points out the unity of the conventional and absolute reality of all universal phenomena is incredible. He really wants us to understand this unity. Lama Tsongkhapa doesn't mention it as such, but I think that unifying the relative and absolute is the most subtle point in the Buddhist teachings. If you don't use his explanation intelligently, however, it will not mean much to you. You need to think deeply about it, read about it, and meditate on it, then gradually you will understand.

☙

Why does Lama Tsongkhapa place such great emphasis on nonduality? In order to discover simultaneously born bliss through inner fire meditation, you must let go of concepts of concrete self-existence. Without some comprehension of nonduality, you may produce heat and bliss, but you will never succeed in inner fire. This is because you will lack wisdom, which means the right view. Most times when we experience bliss, we end up with the wrong view.

Pleasure is not a bad thing in itself; but for most of us it just produces misery and trouble because we lack wisdom. Tantra emphasizes taking pleasure without hesitation, digesting it, and turning it into the great blissful wisdom of nonduality.

We need to be realistic. We live in a fantasy world and fail to touch our fundamental nature. We suffer from a shortage of wisdom. This is why a technique that helps us to touch the fundamental reality of nonduality is most important for us, and why Lama Tsongkhapa emphasizes it here. Through it we can experience everlasting simultaneously born bliss.

We should all practice touching reality in our daily lives. If you meditate for an hour each day, keep at least ten minutes of this time to touch fundamental reality through meditation on emptiness. It is because we lose touch with the fundamental nature of reality that we always find ourselves in emotional situations that we cannot cope with. At the moment we live in a superficial fantasy world, and only when we touch the fundamental nature of reality will we become secure.

In his text on the Guhyasamaja empowerment, Lama Tsongkhapa explains that even though we might not yet have a profound understanding of emptiness, it is sufficient in the beginning to have a gross sense of it as being spacelike in nature. Je Pabongka, a real manifestation of Heruka, also comments that even if we don't have much intellectual understanding of emptiness, it is enough to start with the belief that there is no concrete existence.

Lama Tsongkhapa talks in an earthy way and at our level. Since we do not yet fully understand Nagarjuna's point of view, we have to work at our own level. Lama Tsongkhapa, Je Pabongka, and the other great lamas are very practical. They teach us in a simple way, like teaching a baby, and gradually lead us to perfection.

〜

We should now dedicate our positive energy. "May all sentient beings touch their fundamental nature. May they discover the unity of the relative and absolute characteristics of mind. May they see that all problems appear when they use the unintelligent, narrow mind and that all the mundane puzzles disappear when they use the broad, universal wisdom of nonduality."

PART FOUR

Awakening the Vajra Body

13. Hatha Yoga

After discussing the fundamental characteristics of mind and body, Lama Je Tsongkhapa explains the six physical exercises that are practiced in conjunction with the Six Yogas of Naropa. He briefly mentions vase breathing as the first of the six exercises, then later, just before describing inner fire meditation, he gives a longer explanation of it. I will also explain vase breathing later (see chapter 16).

Now I will talk a little about the exercises, and then I will explain the meditations on the channels, chakras, and syllables. After these preparations, we come to the inner fire meditations themselves, and finally to the experience of the four joys and simultaneously born great blissful wisdom.

These exercises are called the Six Magical Wheels, but I prefer to call them *hatha yoga*. Lama Tsongkhapa states that there are many kinds of hatha yoga exercises associated with the Six Yogas of Naropa, but that the six recommended by Pagmo Drupa are sufficient. These exercises help us to achieve better results from inner fire meditation.

The first of the six exercises is vase breathing, and the remaining five[1] are all practiced while holding the vase breath. It is best to have these exercises demonstrated to you by an experienced teacher. Practicing them after simply reading about them in a book is not a good idea. In ancient times, these practices were kept secret, and they are not even mentioned in the Indian texts. Teaching them publicly to large groups of people was never allowed; they were taught to only one person at a time. It is said that someone who once spied on

Naropa while he was doing these secret exercises lost the sight in one eye as a result.

In order to be successful in inner fire meditation, we need to clean up our nervous system, and these exercises do this by forcefully removing the blockages of energy in the body. They are especially useful for practitioners of inner fire who have done the meditations too strongly. During a retreat, for example, they are practiced in the breaks between meditation sessions. They are also useful for anyone who is meditating a lot and not doing much physical exercise.

Some yogis and yoginis in Tibet performed the exercises naked; others wore a costume a little like a swimsuit. The pants were blue, which is symbolic of Heruka, with a red waistband, symbolic of inner fire. You cannot do the exercises properly in ordinary clothes.

It is best to do the exercises when your stomach feels empty and comfortable. Begin each session by taking refuge, generating bodhicitta, and meditating on Vajrasattva. Then, visualizing Guru Vajradhara and the lineage lamas, meditate on guru yoga and recite the prayer to the lineage lamas.

Arise from emptiness as Heruka with consort. Your light-body is radiant, completely empty, and as clear as crystal. Visualize the three principal channels and the four chakras (see chapter 14). Everything is clean-clear and transparent, and there are no blockages in any of the channels. With this awareness, you then perform the exercises.

Maintaining awareness of yourself as the deity, even while doing these physical exercises, is extremely important. Don't think of yourself as an ordinary person who is just pretending to be the deity. Feel strongly that your body is the deity's body, your speech is the deity's mantra, and your mind is great blissful wisdom. This stops the self-pity mind. Do not lose the divine pride of being this illusory deity, nor your comprehension of yourself as nondual. This makes the exercises very powerful.

Lama Tsongkhapa says that you should hold the vase breath with strong concentration during all the exercises. This is important. If you don't hold your breath during the exercises, you can hurt yourself in various ways. If someone falls from a great height, such as from a five-story building, they won't die or even be badly hurt if they hold their breath in the correct way.

You should breathe slowly, not quickly, during the hatha yoga. Do the vase breathing in a reasonable way, holding your breath according to your ability. If you have to breathe in again at some point during an exercise, breathe through your nostrils, not through your mouth.

In the beginning the exercises may seem difficult, so take your time with them. Doing them too strongly or too quickly will only exhaust you and tax your nervous system. Perform each exercise carefully and correctly, so that it feels blissful. There is no point in rushing through them just to get a reputation for doing all five exercises in one breath. This is not a competition. You are doing something constructive and beneficial, so take your time.

Lama Tsongkhapa says that the body should be loose during the exercises. With practice, your body will eventually become completely flexible, like rubber. This will not happen immediately, of course; but if you do the exercises every day, you will definitely experience the benefits. And remember to shake your body well in the final exercise at the end of the hatha yoga session because this helps the blood to circulate better and the channels to function well.

Some people mistakenly think that it is most important to meditate and to take care of the mind, but that the body is not very important. In tantra, however, the body is as important as the mind because the body has the resource of kundalini energy, and this kundalini-uranium can be harnessed to produce powerful realizations. This is why we have a tantric vow not to criticize or neglect the body. Tantra says that you should take care of your body, keeping it healthy and giving it good food, because you need to have tremendous energy. Giving your body more protein, for example, increases the blissful kundalini power. Respect your body. Don't think that it is just a source of problems. Difficulties come from the mind, not from the body.

When you do the exercises, feel that your negative thoughts and energy blockages are eliminated with each movement and that you feel blissful energy wherever you touch. You can almost see this blissful kundalini energy running through the channels and throughout your entire body of radiant rainbow light. There is no place in your nervous system for pain.

Don't think that blissful energy is found only in the central channel. The kundalini goes to every pore of your body. Imagine that your entire nervous system, from your feet up to your crown, is blissful. There is no space for pain and misery in either your body or your mind. You could say that the purpose of Tibetan yoga is to make it impossible mentally and physically to have space for misery.

A Gelugpa lama wrote that a sign of having gained control over the mind is that the body and its nervous system become conducive to meditation. In other words, your realizations show in the way you coordinate the energy of your body. This is quite impressive, and hatha yoga helps you to accomplish this. The exercises awaken your entire nervous system and bring you bliss twenty-four hours a day. Therefore, the body is definitely something to be respected.

You could say that one of the things you are trying to do when you meditate on inner fire is develop awareness of your body. You are learning to communicate with your own physical energy, especially your heat energy and pleasure energy. You are learning to find the right buttons. The dispensing machines in the West are good examples. You just go to the machine and push the right button. You want Coca-Cola? Here is Coca-Cola. You want coffee? Here is coffee. In a similar way, when you know your own body, you can get whatever you want from it. You don't need to look outside for anything once you have discovered your own pleasure centers and kundalini power.

This is why orgasm is used as a symbol for the experience of everlasting bliss. Lama Tsongkhapa's text mentions this. According to tantra, the resource of orgasm is something good; we can learn from it.

The point of all these physical exercises is to increase desire and blissful kundalini energy, but not for samsaric pleasure. The purpose of these hatha yoga exercises is to help us control the energy of our nervous system during inner fire meditation. When our desire explodes and we are about to lose energy through our sex organ, we should be able to bring the kundalini up from the lower chakras and spread it into the right places. These exercises help us learn how to handle our energy. Eventually we become able to transform our experiences of bliss into wisdom.

Both men and women should learn to work with their desire and control their sexual energy, rather than losing it. This is not just a question of breaking samaya. The point is that we lose the strength of our kundalini energy, and that is not good.

Ordinary physical exercises usually increase superstition, but these hatha yoga exercises can help us to develop nonsuperstitious wisdom. It is possible that while doing one of the exercises, you will simply touch some part of your body and go straight into deep samadhi meditation. Or you will be sitting somewhere relaxing when suddenly your entire body will become blissfully energized. This is not a particularly high realization; it can happen to anyone. You will be doing nothing in particular, and your body will suddenly experience incredible bliss. It should be that way.

Such experiences are possible because of the way these meditations and exercises are structured. They are very profound and very enticing. Ordinary meditation can be boring, but here the meditation object seems to be calling you, "Look! Here is incredible, tantalizing pleasure!"

When Tilopa gave Naropa his first initiation, he simply hit him on the head with his sandal. Naropa instantly went into a deep samadhi. An ordinary person would have been hurt, but Tilopa was shooting at the right target, the crown chakra with its white *ham* syllable. Blissful energy flowed down Naropa's central channel, and he fell into samadhi. This is a good example of the nature of the tantric process. Naropa was struck just once, but instantly entered deep samadhi. It takes great skill for a guru to be able to touch a disciple and evoke such a direct experience. This is initiation. It is powerful and significant, reaching beyond books and somehow beyond even Dharma.

A similar thing happened to Dromtönpa, and he wasn't even physically touched. He suddenly entered a samadhi state while carrying his guru Atisha's feces down some steps. These examples are useful. They have nothing to do with external factors such as meditating in the right physical posture. They are purely inner experiences.

We don't have to look outside for gold. We all have a gold mine within us, in our nervous system. We should just utilize it and be satisfied.

14. Channels and Chakras

Inner fire meditation enables the yogi or yogini to absorb all the energy-winds into the central channel, generate the four joys, and thus experience simultaneously born great blissful wisdom. This process leads to the union of the illusory body and clear light, and finally to full enlightenment.

One of the first practical steps we need to take to achieve this result is to learn about the structure of the vajra body, especially of the channels and chakras. We have to visualize them in meditation until we are totally familiar with them.

To prepare for visualizing the channels and chakras, we need to visualize our body as hollow, or empty. This meditation is simple but very important. When you do it well, there is less chance of experiencing difficulties later when you investigate the channels and chakras. First, however, I will discuss how to sit properly.

❦ SITTING

Marpa said, "None of the Tibetan meditators can compete with me. Just my sitting position is supreme." Marpa had really tasted the Six Yogas of Naropa and was speaking from experience. When you sit, your inner energies should somehow talk to you and bring you bliss. Tantra simply uses the natural resources of your body; it follows your own natural play of energy.

Lama Tsongkhapa states that correct body posture is very important during inner fire meditation. He recommends that you sit on a comfortable seat with your body slightly raised at the back. Cross your legs into the full-lotus position, with your right foot on the left thigh and your left foot on the right thigh. Completion stage practices should be done in this position. It may be difficult for beginners, so just come as close to it as you can. It might also be helpful to use a meditation belt, as Milarepa did, but this is not absolutely necessary.

Your spine should be straight and your head bent slightly forward. Half close your eyes, without focusing on anything, and look toward the tip of your nose. However, if your mind is very distracted and you cannot quiet it, you may find it helpful to close your eyes. Place the tip of your tongue against your palate just behind your front teeth, with your lower jaw relaxed. Your shoulders should be held back straight, not hunched forward. Your hands should be placed below your navel in the mudra of concentration, with the right one on top of the left and with your thumbs touching to form a triangle.

It is especially important to keep your mind and your body a little tight, rather than loose; you can judge from your own experience. You need to train in this. Your body should be upright and slightly tight from the hips to the chest. Most of us slump, and a slumped posture can produce sluggishness. You can recognize yogis and yoginis by the way they hold their bodies.

❧ EMPTY BODY MEDITATION

Visualize yourself as Heruka, standing upright, with your body completely transparent from your head down to your feet. Your body is utterly clear and empty of all material substance, like a balloon filled with air. Nothing at all is inside. Contemplate this.

❧ THE CHANNELS

Once you have become comfortable with seeing your body as empty, you can start to meditate on your channels. First, arise from emptiness in the form of the deity. Your entire body of radiant rainbow light is empty and as clear as crystal; even your hands are like crystal. Heruka's body is not crowded with blood and bones; it is transparent and light. It is a conscious body, a psychic body.

Visualize in front of you your root guru and all the lineage lamas, surrounded by dakas and dakinis. Offer them, without miserliness, your body and the entire world. Then pray to experience blissful air energy, blissful channels, and blissful kundalini. Think, "For the sake of sentient beings, who are as vast in number as the extent of space, I will now engage in this meditation in order to discover Vajradharahood."

Now visualize the three principal channels: the central channel and the right and left channels. They are rainbowlike tubes, smooth, transparent, clear, flexible, and as shiny as silk. The central channel starts at the point midway between the eyebrows, and the side channels start at the nostrils. All three channels curve up to the crown and then run down the length of the body just in front of the spine to end at the tip secret chakra. They are like the central pillar that holds up a roof.

According to the commentary, however, when we do inner fire meditation, we visualize that the three channels end about four finger-widths below the navel, which is the point where we bring the airs into the central channel during the meditation. The side channels curve up into the bottom of the central channel in a shape resembling the Tibetan letter *cha* (ཆ). Lama Tsongkhapa explains how the channels exist in reality and how we should use them in meditation.

He emphasizes that the central channel is close to the spine. It does not actually touch the spine but is very close to it. The side channels are very close to the central channel.

The central channel is blue on the outside, similar to the color of Heruka, and red on the inside. The right channel is red and the left white. When talking about the width of the channels, Tibetans sometimes use the example of a barley straw. I think the plastic drinking straws used in restaurants are also a good example. But in some ways a channel is not like a straw. If you bend a straw when you are drinking a milkshake, it cracks on the outside. Our channels, on the other hand, are as flexible as rubber.

There are also thousands of branch channels within the body, but these three are the main ones that we have to contemplate.

🌿 The chakras

Now let's talk about the various chakras. The four that we utilize most during inner fire meditation are the navel, heart, throat, and crown chakras. We should learn to visualize these four chakras; we should hold our mind on each of them until we eventually penetrate them.

Lama Tsongkhapa says that the navel chakra is red, shaped like a triangle, and has sixty-four branch channels that bend upward from it, rather like the ribs of an upturned umbrella.

The heart chakra is white, shaped like a ball, and has eight branches that point downward toward the navel, like the ribs of an upright umbrella.

The throat chakra is red and also shaped like a ball, with its sixteen branch channels opening upward.

Finally, the great blissful chakra at the crown is multicolored and triangular, and its thirty-two branch channels open downward toward the throat.

The two sets of branch channels opening toward each other in this manner symbolizes method and wisdom. The triangle is symbolic of the wisdom-female energy and the circular shape symbolizes male energy.

I have seen Hindu drawings with a triangle at the navel, just as Lama Tsongkhapa describes here, but sometimes the navel chakra is drawn with a circular shape. My feeling is that the shape is not very important. Use whichever shape you feel comfortable with. Drawings can be useful to demonstrate the chakras and channels. Some Tibetan lamas have made drawings according to their own visions, but these can be difficult to understand because it is not possible to depict exactly what is seen in a vision.

Lama Tsongkhapa explains that in general the branch channels should be visualized as extremely small, but in the beginning it is better to visualize them as having whatever size you find comfortable. If you cannot visualize all the branch channels clearly, simply concentrate on the center of the chakra.

Lama Tsongkhapa also explains that the side channels loop around the central channel at each of the four principal chakras, thus forming knots. There is a sixfold knot at the heart chakra and a twofold knot at each of the other chakras.[1] Some people will not find this easy to visualize. If you find them difficult to visualize, leave out the knots.

𝆃

Where exactly are the chakras? Take the navel chakra, for example. Some texts say that the navel chakra should be visualized directly behind the navel. Lama Tsongkhapa says clearly that the navel chakra is four finger-widths below the navel, where the side channels curve into the central channel. Other texts agree.

This location is quite logical and convincing. When you check, you notice that there is not much feeling at the navel itself, but there is incredible feeling four finger-widths below the navel. However, since the central channel is not located at the front of the body but close to the spine, you should visualize the navel chakra close to the spine. The location of the navel chakra is important because the airs from the two side channels have to enter the central channel exactly at this point.

There are also doubts about the location of the crown chakra, which is also called the bliss chakra. Literally, "crown" refers to the top of the head; therefore, the crown chakra is sometimes said to be between the skin and the skull at the crown of the head. In my opinion, however, this chakra is in the brain, where there is much active energy. This is where the bliss center is located. Some texts call this the head chakra, but we could also call it the brain chakra.

In any case, visualize this chakra somewhere between your eyebrows and your crown, at a point more toward the back of the head. It doesn't need to be in a precisely designated place. We are dealing with psychic reality, not physical reality. However, from your own experience you will slowly discover the exact location within your body of all the chakras. Your practice will then become more precise.

The throat chakra is located directly behind the Adam's apple. The heart chakra is in the center of the chest midway between the two breasts and, again, is more toward the spine than the front of the body.

Although these four are the chakras that we utilize most during inner fire meditation, there are others with which we also need to become familiar. There is a chakra at the brow, midway between the eyebrows. In Western literature this is often referred to as "the third eye." It has six branch channels.

There is also the secret, or sex, chakra. This is red, has thirty-two branches, and is level with the base of the spine. In a man, this is located at the base of the sex organ. As well, there is the middle secret chakra, also known as the jewel chakra, which is white and has eight branch channels; and there is the tip secret chakra, which is at the end of the penis, where the central channel ends.

A question might arise: The secret chakras of the male body are explained very clearly, but what about the female chakras? A woman also has three secret chakras: the secret, middle secret, and tip secret. For a woman, however, these three are hidden inside her body. The tip secret chakra, where her central channel ends, is at the end of the cervix where it opens into the vagina.[2] The man's organ is outside, but the woman's is held inside. As this shows, there is a mutual arrangement between the male's vajra and the female's lotus.

Completion stage tantra also explains that a yogini has a subtle channel that extends from the end of her central channel, and that when the male and female organs join, this subtle channel enters the central channel of the yogi, giving rise to incredible bliss.

We need to develop both clarity and stability in our meditation on the channels and chakras. Begin by concentrating on each one until it appears clearly and then rest within that atmosphere of clarity. By holding the mind at each chakra, we develop stability.

The navel chakra is the most important of the four main chakras because it is the one we focus on during inner fire meditation. In the Six Yogas of Naropa penetrative concentration at the navel chakra is the fundamental step that makes everything else possible, including realization of the illusory body and clear light. It is very quick to bring results.

Concentrating on the navel chakra is also less dangerous than focusing on the secret or heart chakras, for example. Lama Tsongkhapa states that concentrating too much on the heart chakra can cause tension, stress, and even heart problems. Concentrating on the navel chakra is much safer and is fundamental to generating inner fire. Therefore, even when performing the empty body meditations and the hatha yoga exercises, you should pay special attention to the navel chakra.

In the beginning you must meditate on the channels and chakras as described above until you become thoroughly familiar with them.

❦ TRAINING IN THE CHANNELS

Another meditation we should do to prepare for inner fire is to train in the channels; this prevents hindrances and encourages the air energies to enter the central channel. Although it is not mentioned in *Having the Three Convictions*, this technique is recommended by many lamas. As a horse trains for a race, we train ourselves to ride on the wind-energy horse by traveling up and down the central channel investigating everything.

First do the empty body meditation. See yourself as the deity, your light-body as clear as crystal. Visualize the three main channels, all the chakras, and all the branch channels. Everything is transparent, clear, and free from blockages. At the heart chakra visualize a drop of white-red kundalini, the size of a sesame seed. It radiates bright rainbow light of five colors, in nature the five Buddha families.[3]

Concentrate on this drop. Do not look at the drop from the outside. Enter into it, penetrate it, become utterly one with it. Your mind unifies with the drop so that there is no distinction between subject and object. Within this blissful atmosphere of being the drop, you are no longer attracted to any sensory objects. Everything is set up for you to do deep meditation.

You, as the energy drop, look down from the heart chakra and see the navel and secret chakras. You then look up and see the throat, crown, and brow chakras. The passage of the central channel is clear. You go up through the passage and reach the throat chakra. Looking around, you see clearly all its sixteen branch channels.

You then move up to the crown chakra, which has thirty-two branch channels, and you see all of them clearly. Next you go to the brow chakra, which opens outside at the point midway between your eyebrows. From here you look at your Heruka body, which is of radiant blue light and in the nature of nonduality. You see everything clearly all the way down to the feet. You feel extremely blissful.

From the brow chakra you go back into the central channel to the crown chakra and look down at the throat chakra. Again go to the throat and observe its sixteen branch channels. Go down to the heart and look at the eight branch channels there. Continue down to the navel and see clearly each of the sixty-four branch channels. Next investigate the secret chakra, the jewel chakra, and finally the tip secret chakra. Finally, return to the heart. Make the journey up and down the central channel many times, always ending up at the heart chakra.

You should not be concerned that visualizing the three channels continuing down below the navel in this way will conflict with the inner fire meditations. Here we are simply investigating everything as preparation for the inner fire meditations. In any case, later when we practice the four joys, we will need to visualize the central channel going all the way down to the lower chakras.

Meditate in this way until you are completely familiar with your channels and chakras. Eventually, you will know exactly where everything is, just as you know where everything is in your purse.

Imagine that as you travel up and down the central channel, the rainbow light of the kundalini drop helps to regenerate and activate the channels. Blocked channels are opened, crooked channels are straightened, and wrinkled ones are smoothed. Everything becomes rainbowlike. All the channels become as soft as silk, transparent, and serviceable, almost as if they would do anything you tell them to do.

When you do this meditation, you should not keep your concentration for too long at the heart chakra. As I mentioned earlier, Lama Tsongkhapa warns that staying too long at the heart chakra can create dangerous tension. In fact, you should also not spend much time at the throat or crown chakras. Because we are preparing ourselves for inner fire meditation, our main emphasis should be on the navel chakra.

If you have meditated well on your body as empty, there is no need to worry about experiencing pain in your channels or chakras when you travel through them. The point of doing the empty-body visualization is to prevent such problems. When you do have some pain in your body, you don't need to ask anyone what to do about it. Lama Tsongkhapa has already given you the solution.

Now let's dedicate the merit: "By meditating on the three main channels and the four main chakras, may we loosen the tightness of the blocked channels. May all the wind energy enter the central channel, and may we thereby experience the path of clear light. By penetrating the pleasure centers of the chakras, may we achieve the realization of the eternal state of bliss."

15. Blissful Syllables

Remember that you have a body of radiant rainbow light in the form of Heruka. It is not crowded with blood and bones, but is empty and has clear channels and chakras that are free from all blockages and confusion. In the previous meditation, you traveled to all the chakras and investigated their structure. You are now ready to put a seed-syllable in the center of each of the four main chakras. This will be your object of concentration.

Lama Tsongkhapa says that placing seed-syllables in the chakras is vital to generating the four blisses. Eventually, when the kundalini at our crown chakra melts and flows down the central channel, because we have already concentrated on the letters at each chakra, we will be able to hold the kundalini longer at each point. We will thus intensify the experiences of bliss there.

You should place the letters right in the center of the four principal chakras. The syllables should be visualized as small and as subtle as possible, the size of a mustard or sesame seed. Lama Tsongkhapa emphasizes that they should be subtle. This encourages the airs to enter automatically into the central channel and to absorb strongly. Because of this, your concentration will be stronger, and you will therefore generate stronger bliss.

First we place a syllable in the navel chakra. We put there the *short a*, or in Tibetan *a tung* (see next page), which looks like the final stroke of the Tibetan letter *a* (ཨ). The *short a* is broad at the bottom and then thins to become very sharp at the tip. You can also visualize it as a candle flame or a *torma*, both of which are broad at the bottom and fine at the top. Remember, however, that it is very subtle.

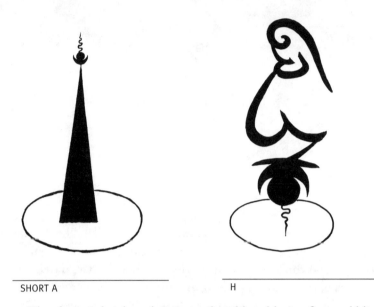

Calligraphy by Lama Zopa Rinpoche

SHORT A   H

The *short a* is bright red. It is very hot, like a blazing fire, and bliss-ful in nature. At its tip are a crescent moon, a drop, and a fine, sharp nada. (*Nada* is a Sanskrit term that sometimes refers to nonduality, so perhaps we could say it means "nondual top.")

Some lamas say that the *short a* stands on a sun disk, but Lama Tsongkhapa recommends visualizing it on a moon disk. Since we are trying to generate inner heat, it would seem more logical to visualize the *short a* on a sun disk. My feeling is that Lama Tsongkhapa decided it should be on a moon disk to help prevent the arising of ordinary inner heat, which is superficial and momentary.

Place the *short a* right inside the central channel in the center of the navel chakra, which is located four finger-widths below the navel. Lama Tsongkhapa clearly states that the *short a* should be in the navel chakra and in the central channel. Other lamas agree that the *short a* is to be visualized at the point where the side channels join the central channel, but they say that the navel chakra is at the navel itself. Also, many texts advise us to put the concentration object in the chakra, but they do not expressly say to put it in the central channel. Lama Tsongkhapa says that it is vital to find the correct location, because this is the exact point at which the airs enter the central channel through the two side channels.

O   A

Lama Tsongkhapa also emphasizes that we should visualize the *short a* closer to the spine than to the front of the body. He repeats this again and again. Locating the *short a* here helps the inner heat to grow in a proficient and profound way and stops the arising of ordinary heat. His Holiness Trijang Rinpoche also said that visualizing the syllables closer to the spine allows the inner heat to grow more gradually, strongly, and profoundly. It is not good to have the heat rise extremely quickly, like an explosion.

Next place a blue *hūṃ,* with a crescent moon, drop, and nada on a moon disc at the heart chakra. The whole thing is upside down. The normal way of writing *hūṃ* in Tibetan is rather complicated, so you can visualize it in a simplified form, similar to the *short a.* At the very least you could visualize a blue light that is wider at the top and finer at the bottom. Our eventual aim is, with single-pointed concentration, to energize the dripping of blissful kundalini down through the syllable and the nada. This blue *hūṃ* communicates with the red *short a* at the navel.

Now visualize a moon disk at the throat chakra and on it a red *oṃ.* Alternatively, you can visualize a red *aṃ.* Both syllables are acceptable. You can also visualize the *oṃ* in a simplified form. Just use the *a* part of the *oṃ* if that is easier for you. This red syllable stands

HA

upright and has a crescent moon, drop, and nada above it. Again, it should be visualized in the central channel, right in the center of the throat chakra.

At the crown, which is the chakra of great bliss, we place a white *ham* on a moon disk. You can also simplify this syllable to a hooklike shape. It has a crescent, a drop, and a nada, and again, the whole thing is upside down. It communicates with the red *om* at the throat.

Contemplate each of these four syllables in turn, but focus mainly on the *short a* at the navel. When you contemplate the *short a* (and the other syllables), your consciousness should completely unify with it. It looks so enticing that you just want to merge with it. Lama Tsongkhapa states that we should not see the syllable "out there" and ourselves separate from it. Instead, we should become completely unified with each syllable.

All the letters should be very bright and in the nature of kundalini. Lama Tsongkhapa says that they drip with kundalini, like dew. Visualizing the letters as bright and radiant prevents sluggishness and sleepiness; it leaves no room for mental darkness. Seeing them as blissful automatically eliminates the distracted, wandering mind, which comes from dissatisfaction. Everything is set up to help us to develop deep concentration.

Lama Tsongkhapa points out that when you meditate on the syllables your concentration should not be too tense or too loose, but somewhere in between. He also mentions other techniques, such as placing syllables in the branch channels, but this is not necessary for now. The meditation I have given above is the most important.

Although in general the syllables should be visualized as small as possible, Lama Tsongkhapa says that in the beginning it is acceptable to visualize them as large. As you progress in your meditation you can then gradually reduce them in size.

What are the benefits of contemplating the concentration objects at the chakras? Contemplating the *ham* at the crown increases the white male kundalini, which is the source of bliss. Contemplating and penetrating the *om* at the throat chakra increases the female blood energy and also helps the practice of dream yoga. Concentrating on the *hūm* at the heart helps to develop the clear light. And meditating on the *short a* at the navel increases the strength of the inner fire; it also increases the white blissful energy, because of the navel chakra's link with the left channel. Activating inner heat at the navel chakra automatically causes energy to come to the crown chakra. Simply touching the area below your navel, you will feel a sensation at your crown.

While we should become familiar with all the chakras, remember that the inner fire at the navel is the key to the realizations of all of the chakras.

Different tantras utilize the navel chakra, as well as the chakras at the upper and lower openings of the central channel, in different ways. Lama Tsongkhapa actually describes these earlier in *Having the Three Convictions*, in the section on the characteristics of the body, but I have chosen to discuss them here.

According to Marpa's tradition, there are two periods for practicing the tantric yogas: when we are awake and when we are asleep. Sutrayana practice uses only the waking state, but Highest Yoga Tantra has ways to utilize the sleeping state as well.

Marpa explains that the heart and throat chakras are key points for sleep yoga and that the navel and crown chakras are for practices during the waking state. During the waking state, the navel chakra is important for the practice of inner fire and the crown chakra for consort practice. This is because at these times the subtle energy drops abide at each of these points.

Lama Tsongkhapa also discusses the view of the Kalachakra Tantra, which says that the navel and brow chakras are associated with waking state practices and that the throat and secret chakras are important for practice during dreams.

Lama Tsongkhapa then gives his own views. He says that as we go to sleep, the winds gather strongly at the heart and jewel chakras and that we remain in deep sleep as long as they remain there. (The drops and winds also gather strongly at the jewel chakra when we are in deep sleep; this is why men sometimes ejaculate then.) During heavy sleep we do not dream. Once the sleep becomes lighter the winds also become lighter; they gather at the secret and throat chakras, and at that time dreams come. When the air energies move to the brow and navel chakras, we wake up.

Even though these chakras are fundamental to practice during sleep and dream states, this does not mean that they are not important during the waking state as well. Lama Je Tsongkhapa says that penetrating and contemplating each chakra brings its own particular results and realizations. In the system of practice of the Six Yogas of Naropa, however, everything is approached through the navel chakra.

In all the meditations on the channels and chakras, we are advised to visualize them as clear and rainbowlike. In reality, however, at the moment they are not like that at all. Our side channels adhere to the central channel, squeezing and blocking it. The channels are often shriveled and wrinkled, and there is much crowding and confusion at the chakras where all the smaller channels branch out. How are the chakras loosened and opened so that the air energies can enter the central channel? How do the channels become clear and rainbowlike?

The basic principle is that the mind, and therefore the wind energies that always accompany it, automatically go to whatever point the mind contemplates. Concentration on the vital points thus gradually clarifies and unblocks the channels and chakras. This creates space for the subtle energies to flow, similar to the way that blowing air into a balloon causes it to open and expand.

When you penetrate the navel chakra, for example, the blockages are released, the chakra opens, and the winds automatically enter the central channel. The same thing happens at the heart and at the other chakras. In fact, contemplating the *short a* at the navel also automatically energizes the heart chakra, which is squeezed by its branch channels. Wind comes up from the navel chakra and pushes the heart chakra open. This automatically energizes and opens the throat and crown chakras as well.

Penetrative concentration on the chakras, however, always brings some tension in the beginning. The wind energy gathers where the mind focuses, and sometimes the winds move the wrong way and produce physical and emotional pain. This happens if we have not prepared well, which is why the empty-body meditation, the vase breathing, the hatha yoga exercises, and the meditations on the channels, chakras, and syllables are all essential preparations for inner fire meditation.

At the moment our channels are crowded, tense, and constricted, and it takes time to loosen them. Even though the channels are subtle phenomena, they nonetheless have form. When we do the meditations on the channels, chakras, and syllables again and again, our channels become unblocked, clean-clear, functional, and as soft as silk. If we make these preparations, when we meditate on inner heat and eventually penetrate the vital points at the chakras, the air can easily enter and completely absorb into the central channel.

You should alternate the various practices because they support each other. Eventually, you will develop a feeling of unity, almost as if your bodily energy is consciousness and your consciousness is bodily energy. Your body and mind will cooperate perfectly with each other.

When you are feeling much devotion, it is good to pray to all the lineage lamas for blessings to receive the realizations of all the meditations. Visualize them in your heart chakra, like a tiny reflection in a crystal. All universal phenomena are also reflected there. Alternatively, you can simply visualize Naropa in your heart chakra.

With devotion, you then pray, "May I be successful in inner fire meditation. May my entire nervous system experience an explosion of blissful energy. May all this blissful energy enter the central channel, and may it comprehend the wisdom of nonduality."

16. Vase Breathing Meditation

As I mentioned earlier, *Having the Three Convictions* lists vase breathing meditation as the first of the six hatha yoga exercises, although Lama Tsongkhapa describes it only briefly in that section.

Vase breathing is not an insignificant practice. The other five hatha yoga exercises are performed while holding the vase breath, and, most important, the inner fire meditations are performed on the basis of this breathing technique. Successfully bringing all the airs into the central channel and stabilizing and absorbing them there depend upon vase breathing.

❧ DISPELLING THE IMPURE AIRS

Before attempting to practice vase breathing, you should first dispel all the impure airs with the nine-round breathing exercise.

Holding your left nostril closed with the back of your right index finger, breathe in slowly through your right nostril. Then block your right nostril with the front of the same finger and exhale through your left nostril. Think that you are breathing out all your impure desire energy. Do this three times. Actually, you don't need to hold the nostril closed; you can just visualize the air leaving through the other nostril.

Now do the reverse, breathing in three times through the left nostril. As you exhale through your right nostril, think that you are breathing out all your impure hatred energy. Finally, breathe in and out three times through both nostrils to make all the energies clean-clear and equal. As you exhale, think that you are breathing out all your impure ignorance energy. In total this makes nine rounds.[1]

Lama Tsongkhapa emphasizes that you should breathe in and out only through your nostrils, not through your mouth. He recommends breathing in first through the right nostril, but because the female principle of mother tantra is normally associated with the left side, you might want to emphasize the auspiciousness of female energy by breathing in first through your left nostril. If you want to emphasize the father tantra approach, breathe in first through your right nostril.

Breathe in slowly and gently. While breathing in, you can think you are inhaling pure blissful energy from Tilopa, Naropa, and all the Buddhas and bodhisattvas of the ten directions. When you exhale, think that all your physical and mental difficulties, the symptoms of your blocked energy, disappear. This is not simply visualization. As soon as you begin to practice nine-round breathing, you will feel some change. When exhaling, first breathe out gently, then strongly, and then gently again.

❦ VASE BREATHING

Ideally, you should practice vase breathing when your stomach is empty and comfortable; in other words, before eating a meal or after the food has been digested. Posture is also important. Your body should be very straight; vase breathing cannot be effective if your body is bent and squeezed.

The vase breathing meditation comprises four steps: inhaling; filling the right and left channels with air; milking the air from the two side channels into the central channel; and exhaling, or "shooting up like an arrow."

Begin the practice by making your hands into vajra fists: place the tip of the thumb at the base of the ring finger and then close the four fingers over the thumb. Place your hands on top of your thighs, with your arms very close to your body and locked straight. Stretch your body upward as much as possible; this enables the airs to flow better. However, you don't have to sit like this all the time; after a while, you can sit normally.

Visualize yourself as the deity and visualize clearly the three main channels and four principal chakras as described earlier. Concentrate on the *short a* in the navel chakra.

The first step is inhaling. Breathe in slowly and gently through both nostrils until your lungs are completely filled, visualizing that the air is filling the two side channels. Remember not to inhale through your mouth and to bring in a complete breath. Although some lamas say to breathe in strongly, Lama Tsongkhapa emphasizes that the inhalation should be very slow and very gentle.

In the second step, visualize that the right and left channels are filled with air, like inflated balloons.

With the third step, while holding the breath, you swallow a little saliva, tense your diaphragm, and press firmly down. Feel that these downward movements push the inhaled air all the way down the two side channels to the *short a* at your navel chakra. You might need to exert a little force to hold the air there.

Then, still holding your breath and pressing down with the diaphragm, tighten the lower doors by contracting your pelvic muscles. This brings up the lower airs to embrace and unify with the upper airs at the navel chakra. Feel that the *short a* is magnetizing the air energies, drawing them all into the central channel. Imagine that the upper and lower airs unite precisely at the *short a*,[2] which is in the central channel in the navel chakra. (The reason this breathing technique is called vase meditation is that the *short a* is held by the upper and lower airs as if it were in a vase or a teapot.) Hold your breath and tense the upper and lower muscles for as long as you can.

Don't think that the process is complicated or that you will have difficulty doing it. Many things seem to be happening at the same time, but the main steps involve bringing the airs from above and below and unifying them at the navel chakra. Rather than forcing the process, you should feel that the *short a* automatically draws all the airs into the navel chakra. Good concentration helps all this to happen naturally.

Finally, we come to the fourth step. When you can no longer comfortably hold your breath, you should exhale through your nostrils, visualizing that the unified upper and lower airs held at the *short a* shoot up the central channel like an arrow. They completely absorb inside the central channel, energizing much bliss.

You should exhale slowly at first, but toward the end of the expiration breathe the air out forcefully until your lungs feel empty. Although Lama Tsongkhapa's text does not mention to breathe out strongly (in fact, he advises us to release the breath gently and quietly), I have seen many lamas do it this way.

While some lamas say that you should visualize the air leaving the body at the crown, Lama Tsongkhapa says that it should be kept inside the central channel. This is understandable since our main aim is to have all the winds enter, stabilize, and be absorbed there. From the navel chakra the air goes to the heart, throat, and then crown, but it does not exit from the crown chakra.

❦

Although we visualize all the air going into the two side channels when we breathe in, our purpose is to fill the central channel, not the side channels. In order to accomplish this, we bring the air down completely and hold it below the navel, where the side channels enter the central channel. When we swallow saliva and then milk the airs from the side channels into the central channel at the navel chakra, the central channel automatically opens, and all the airs from the side channels enter into it.

When the side channels are open and functioning, the central channel is closed; and when the central channel is open and functioning, the side channels are closed. Lama Tsongkhapa says that these are the only alternatives.

According to Lama Tsongkhapa's experience, holding the unified upper and lower airs at the navel chakra can be uncomfortable in the beginning, with the abdomen sometimes becoming a little bloated. He explains, however, that with practice the discomfort passes and the abdomen naturally shrinks.

Some people might feel that they cannot bring the airs from above and below to unify at the navel chakra; others might feel that their abdomen is too small. The solution is not to force anything. Don't rush to unify the two airs. Of course, it is a good idea to apply a little force at the beginning, but not so much that you have difficulty or pain. Don't think that you can only do this practice forcefully. Just try to bring the energy inside in a relaxed fashion.

If you don't like to do the meditation forcefully, imagine that the *short a* itself magnetically attracts the airs from above and below, drawing them into union at the navel chakra. It is as if the *short a* sucks the entire energy of your body into the navel chakra. Without any effort, you visualize that the *short a* forcefully draws the airs from the two side channels, as well as from all the other channels, and from above and below, into one unified absorption. This is an easy way to do vase meditation.

If you apply too much force, you may experience wind disorders, known as *lung* in Tibetan. You could also experience strong heart palpitations, suffer cold sweats, or feel sick. Don't strain. Just practice in a relaxed and natural way. Perform the technique slowly and gently, and allow the process to develop in accordance with your personal capacity. Everyone's body is different. Some people have large stomachs, others small; some have large channels, others small. Everyone should breathe according to their individual proportions. In any case, the process is the same.

In my opinion, Lama Tsongkhapa is saying that each individual person can judge how much air to bring in and how long to hold it. A lama can instruct you in the techniques, but you should decide from your own experience what works best for you.

The more gently you go in the beginning, the more forcefully you will eventually be able to bring all the airs to the navel chakra. Lama Tsongkhapa says, however, that at a certain point vase breathing will come naturally. As your concentration becomes stable, you will find that you can hold the upper and lower winds together effortlessly and naturally. You might be finding the technique difficult, but then suddenly and unexpectedly one day your breathing will become more natural, more subtle, and more easily controlled. You will be able to tell from your own experiences when you have succeeded.

You might not be meditating, simply talking or doing some ordinary activity, yet you suddenly notice that you are doing vase breathing. You press down a little, and the energies spontaneously move around inside your body. With regular practice the process becomes very natural, and you will find yourself bringing the airs inside automatically.

Of course, if you really do find the technique too complicated, just breathe naturally and develop concentration on the *short a*. Lama Tsongkhapa's commentary actually says that vase breathing is not absolutely required for success in the inner fire meditations. You can breathe with small natural breaths, yet deep down you hold the energies.

Holding the upper and lower winds together at the navel chakra is the key to success in inner fire meditation. You should practice vase breathing over and over again, until you can do it effortlessly. It is not a difficult technique; in fact, it is unbelievably easy. A sense of bliss arising from the secret chakra will indicate that you are making progress. Even performing the vase meditation without much concentration will induce bliss. You don't need to be a great meditator. All you have to do is practice, live peacefully, control yourself, relax, and you can experience blissful energy even without good concentration.

Vase breathing can also be used as a way to extend your life span. It is said that each of us takes a fixed number of breaths during our life, and if we can learn to control our usual rapid breathing and breathe more slowly, we can prolong our life.

Also, I think that slowing the rhythm of our breathing slows down our nervous system, and then our mind automatically slows down as well. In this way our concentration spontaneously becomes much stronger and our mind less distracted.

There are various ways to assess your progress in vase breathing. Kagyu practitioners have a method of timing the vase breath in which you touch one knee, then the other, then your forehead, and finally snap your fingers three times. This cycle is counted as one unit of measurement. Being able to do 108 of these while holding a vase breath is considered a sign of great success; seventy-two indicates middling success; and thirty-six, small success. The Kagyu texts explain that this success is only from the point of view of a beginner. For advanced yogis and yoginis, there is no question of counting; they can hold their breath for an extremely long time.

Lama Tsongkhapa has a different way of counting. You place your right palm on the left palm and stroke it three times, touch both knees, then snap your fingers six times. The Kagyu method seems simpler to me. Concentrating deeply on inner fire and performing complicated counting at the same time would be difficult. I do not negate Lama Tsongkhapa's method. I'm sure that someone with indestructible concentration could count in his way; but those who are easily distracted would find it better to count by the other method. There were no watches or clocks in the old days, so time couldn't be calculated accurately. Anyway, these days we all have watches so we don't need to count in either Lama Tsongkhapa or Kagyupa style. We can count in twentieth-century style.

We should now dedicate the merit. "May the hatred and desire energy from the right and left channels totally absorb into the *short a*. May all sentient beings experience the wind energies entering into the central channel, becoming stable, and then absorbing there. May they all discover the clear light."

PART FIVE

Discovering Totality

17. Inner Fire Meditation

According to Lama Je Tsongkhapa's commentary, when we are proficient in the vase breathing meditation and our concentration is reasonable, we can approach inner fire meditation. This produces the real inner fireworks. At this point we should already be thoroughly familiar with the syllables in the chakras: the *short a, hūṃ, oṃ,* and *haṃ.* These syllables should be visualized in the central channel, clean-clear in their own individual colors and radiating light. On the basis of vase meditation and visualizing these syllables, we then do the more technical inner fire meditations.

Inner fire is a very special and distinguished tantric technique. I mentioned earlier that some lamas in ancient times said that the meditations of the evolutionary stage are not necessary and are only used for gaining worldly realizations. In a sense they are right. I'm joking, of course; they are wrong. But I want you to see my point. The completion stage practice of inner fire is like shooting a rocket along a completely straight path. It deals only with what is essential. By comparison, the evolutionary stage is like dreaming.

As I said earlier, inner fire is the root of success in all completion stage practices. It is the perfect method for awakening our very subtle consciousness, whose function is to comprehend the totality of nonduality wisdom. This completion stage experience of simultaneously born great blissful wisdom is the ultimate result of inner fire meditation.

Lama Je Tsongkhapa says, "By practicing inner fire, you can easily bring the wind energies into the central channel and easily develop the four joys. From that experience you can then meditate on clear light and the illusory body." He continues, "All the methods for bringing the wind energies into the central channel and for energizing these four states of bliss are based on inner fire meditation."

The simultaneously born wisdom *mahamudra* comes from the four joys. These in turn come from inner fire meditation, which depends on the airs entering the central channel. Without these auspicious tantric methods, enlightenment cannot be actualized.

Experiences of clarity, bliss, and nonsuperstitious, indestructible samadhi are common to Hinayana, Paramitayana, and Tantrayana. However, there is a big difference between the nonsuperstitious wisdom of Hinayana and Paramitayana and the blissful, simultaneously born wisdom of tantra. Lama Tsongkhapa points this out very clearly.

Inner fire meditation is the most powerful way to achieve blissful, indestructible samadhi. This is illustrated by the story I mentioned earlier of the first meeting between Gampopa and Milarepa. Gampopa told Milarepa that he had such deep samadhi meditation that he could meditate for many days without distraction or sluggishness. Milarepa simply laughed and said, "I'm not impressed by that! Dear son, there is no comparison between my tummo *short a* and your indestructible samadhi meditation. I don't know why you're so proud of it. You cannot get olive oil by squeezing sand. My inner fire meditation is incomparable."

Milarepa was not speaking out of egotistical pride. Inner fire meditation is very special. As Milarepa put it, sitting for many days in a conventional samadhi is like trying to get oil by squeezing sand. This is impossible. Inner fire meditation, however, quickly produces the real oil.

Milarepa is talking from his own experience. Inner fire meditation is far more effective than ordinary deep meditation. It quickly grows into an explosion of nonduality wisdom, an explosion of telepathic power, an explosion of realizations. It is the key to countless treasures.

Why is inner fire meditation such a powerful way to achieve blissful samadhi? First, its meditation object is not external, but inside your own body. Second, it is located in the central channel. Third, it is located not only in the central channel but specifically in the navel chakra.

The various tantras have their own methods for bringing the airs into the central channel. In inner fire meditation the approach is made through the navel chakra. Although inner fire can also be approached through the crown, throat, or heart chakras, it is easier and safer to bring the airs into the central channel at the navel chakra.

Lama Tsongkhapa describes the navel chakra as being triangular in shape. You can perhaps think of it as a pyramid. Focusing on the concentration object, the *short a*, which is you yourself, in this pyramid leads to indestructible concentration. There is no movement and no distraction. Penetrative concentration at the navel chakra is the foundation that makes everything else possible.

A fourth point that makes inner fire special is that it generates such incredible bliss that your mind simply wants to stay at the pleasure center at your navel. It has no desire to go outside to anything else. Inner fire burns up your dissatisfied energy, bringing you total physical and psychological satisfaction.

In any case, how can your mind move from the navel chakra once the vase meditation has forcefully brought the winds to the *short a*? Your mind rides on the wind, so if the vehicle is not moving, the mind cannot go anywhere. It has no choice; it has to stay there. In this way, with inner fire meditation we quickly attain indestructible samadhi.

❧ PREPARING FOR INNER FIRE

As I mentioned earlier, your stomach should be empty and comfortable when you do the inner fire meditation. Also, you need to keep your posture erect so that the energy of your entire body is strong. Your meditation will not work if you have a sloppy posture. Keeping your body upright and slightly tensed brings about unity and communication from the toes to the crown.

Start the meditation by dissolving yourself and everything else into emptiness, and then arise from emptiness in the form of Heruka. Strongly identify with being the deity, having a body of radiant blue light, a rainbow body, or a crystal body. Recognize that you, Heruka, are a reflection of the simultaneously born wisdom of nonduality.

Suddenly Guru Vajradhara appears in the space of nonduality in front of you. He is embracing his consort, and their bodies of radiant blue light energize you with great bliss. Recognize Guru Vajradhara as the deity, the daka and the dakini, and the Dharma protector.

Vajradhara is surrounded by the lineage gurus of the Six Yogas of Naropa: Tilopa, Naropa, Marpa, Milarepa, Gampopa, Lama Tsong-khapa, and the others. These great beings completed the practice; they achieved the inner fire realization and discovered the totality of the illusory body and clear light wisdom. They energize us and give us great inspiration to develop the realization of inner fire. We offer all our experiences of blissful sensory energy to the lineage gurus and to the dakas and dakinis, enhancing the great bliss within them.

Then strongly and single-pointedly pray, "May all mother sentient beings discover their great blissful channels and chakras. May they bring great blissful wind energy into the central channel, and stabilize and absorb it there. May all sentient beings discover the blissful kundalini power of simultaneously born great wisdom." Generate the motivation to discover the totality of Vajradharahood, the union of the illusory body and clear light. In order to achieve this totality, you are now going to practice the yoga of inner fire.

All the lineage gurus dissolve into Vajradhara, who then energizes bliss within you by sending radiant white light into your crown chakra, radiant red light into your throat chakra, and radiant blue light into your heart chakra.

Next focus on your crown chakra. It is clear of all blockages. Penetrate the syllable *ham,* with its crescent moon, drop, and nada on top. It is white in color, on a moon disk, and upside down. See the *ham* clearly inside the central channel in the center of the chakra.

White light radiates from the *ham* and totally fills your crown chakra. All darkness and nonfunctional energy are eliminated. Every cell of your brain is awake and active, energizing bliss and peace. Both the crown chakra and the syllable *ham* give you great blissful energy.

At your throat chakra on a moon disk is a radiant red *om* with a crescent moon, drop, and nada. The red *om* at the throat chakra and the white *ham* at the crown communicate with each other, arousing the unity of bliss and nonduality. Feel that this communication opens, unties, and loosens the blocked channels. Again, both the throat chakra and its syllable give you great blissful energy.

At the heart chakra on a moon disk is an upside down blue *hūm* with a crescent moon, drop, and nada. The *hūṃ* radiates infinite, blissful, blue light. The blue *hūṃ* at the heart communicates with the *short a* below your navel.

Standing on a moon disk, the *short a* is bright red, blissful in character, and incredibly hot. It is also adorned with a crescent moon, a drop, and a nada, which is very fine and sharp. The *short a* is your main concentration object. Penetrate it, so that subject and object are unified. Your consciousness becomes the *short a* and the *short a* becomes your consciousness.

The *short a* should be bright, and the hotter it gets, the brighter it becomes. Seeing the syllable as radiant eliminates sluggishness, which is characterized by darkness and lack of clarity; and seeing it as blissful prevents your mind from wandering. Eventually, the psychological satisfaction that comes from the bliss will stop all distracted thoughts.

❦

There are four technical meditations to help you to attain the realization of inner fire: igniting the inner fire, blazing the inner fire, blazing and dripping, and extraordinary blazing and dripping.

❧ IGNITING THE INNER FIRE

Begin with the vase meditation. Breathe in gently, slowly, and completely through both nostrils. Feel the air filling the side channels. You can visualize the air as blue or smoke-colored if you like. Also, imagine that air is drawn in through all the pores of your Heruka body, not just through your nostrils.

Swallow a little saliva, and with that downward movement, press the air down to the navel chakra. Then tighten the muscles of your lower doors so that the lower air comes up to the navel chakra to unify with the upper air.

The *short a,* which is your consciousness, has the magnetic power to draw into itself not only the wind from the right and left channels but also the wind from all the pores of your body, from the upper and lower chakras, and from all the ten directions. Be sure to visualize this because it will give you a strong feeling that the winds have actually entered the central channel.

The airs heat the *short a* intensely, just as blowing on a coal fire makes it hotter and hotter. The *short a* becomes very bright and super-hot. The hotter it becomes, the more blissful your psychic energy, which is unified with the *short a,* becomes.

When you need to exhale, do so strongly and completely, but visualize that all the air shoots up the central channel and is absorbed there.

Maintaining awareness of yourself as one with the *short a,* once again breathe in slowly, gently, and completely through both nostrils. Swallow and push down. Feel that all your emotional, self-pity energy from the right and left channels is magnetically sucked into and burnt up in the *short a.* Tighten the lower muscles to bring the lower airs up to the navel chakra and unify them there with the airs brought down through the side channels.

Focus with penetrative awareness on the *short a.* Feel the heat intensify and the *short a* begin to blaze. It remains the same size, but a flame shoots up from it, then dies down again. The blissful heat automatically keeps your attention absorbed in the *short a.* Contemplate this and let go.

Repeat the vase meditation, but without pushing. Allow the process to happen naturally. Concentrate strongly on being one with the *short a* and intensify the inner fire.

Brilliant red light from the *short a* now radiates up the central channel to embrace the heart, throat, and crown chakras. From the crown of your head all the way down to your feet, your entire Heruka body is filled with blissful, radiant red light.

The heat that arises from this meditation should not be superficial and gross but deep and initially subtle. This is the character of the inner heat we are trying to generate. If you push the meditation in such a way that you perspire, you are not producing the right inner heat. If the heat arises slowly in the beginning, the right results will follow.

Concentrate with penetrative awareness on the *short a*; the blissful heat will keep your attention right there. Don't intellectualize. Simply contemplate and let go. All that exists is blissful awareness of the *short a.*

❧ BLAZING THE INNER FIRE

Having ignited the inner fire, we can now begin to cause it to blaze. Again the basis of the practice is the vase meditation. Your consciousness is utterly unified with the *short a*. Breathe in deeply and imagine that all your emotional desire and hatred are drawn magnetically and powerfully down the side channels with the incoming air. This absorbs into the *short a* and is burned up by the inner fire.

Swallow and press down firmly. Tighten your lower muscles so that the lower winds are drawn up to touch and unify with the upper winds at the *short a*. Like a magnet, the *short a* at the navel draws all the winds to itself. The *short a,* which is your consciousness, is supersensitive and superhot. The hotter it becomes, the greater your experience of bliss.

The *short a* becomes so overheated by the winds that the inner fire explodes, blazing up three or four inches inside the central channel. Previously the flame was small and lasted only a moment; now it is powerful and doesn't die down. Because of the brilliance of the inner fire, you can see your entire body from your position within the navel chakra. The blissful heat shoots up the central channel and automatically stimulates the other chakras. The syllables there are on the point of melting into blissful kundalini nectar.

Keeping your concentration within the blazing *short a,* hold your breath for as long as it is comfortable. Then exhale and imagine that all the winds shoot up the central channel. Experience bliss. Now tighten your lower muscles slightly. This is like adding bliss: you experience more blissful energy and more explosions of heat.

Repeat the process again. Completely breathe in new air, press down, tighten the lower muscles, and at the same time penetrate the *short a*. The upper and lower winds are magnetically drawn to the *short a*. They curve around it, causing the inner fire to blaze and to generate incredible heat. The more heat there is, the more response you will feel at your heart, throat, and crown chakras. Feel the *hūṃ* at the heart vibrate; it is about to melt. There is also some response at the *oṃ* at your throat and the *haṃ* at your crown. Blissful kundalini is about to drip down from them.

Every movement of energy is encouraging your consciousness to unify with bliss and with universal reality. The more penetrating your awareness of yourself as the *short a,* the more you touch totality. Your consciousness goes beyond gross concepts to become subtle, clear, and deep.

Remember that it is not possible to be Heruka and still have ordinary energy flowing through your body. Your entire rainbow body is filled with heat, kundalini, and great bliss. You are totally aware, superconscious, and this subtle awareness touches universal reality.

❧ Blazing and Dripping

Once again perform the vase breathing meditation. The universal wind energy is magnetically drawn from all directions into the *short a,* causing it to generate superheat. The wrongly directed negative energies of the right and left channels are no longer functioning. These winds have dissolved, and fresh, positive energy is produced in the central channel. Feel the new movement of air energy coming into your navel chakra. This fresh wind energy is the resource of inner heat, intensifying the inner fire and melting the kundalini.

Focus with penetrative awareness on the *short a.* The inner fire explodes into a flame that blazes all the way up to your heart chakra, bringing you much bliss. The fire wraps around the blue *hūṃ* at your heart three times, and the heart chakra and the *hūṃ* become super-hot. The heart chakra fills with blissful kundalini, which flows downward from the *hūṃ* and the moon disk and drips from the tip of the *hūṃ* onto the *short a.* This is like pouring liquid butter onto a fire. The inner fire explodes with superheat. Your entire nervous system becomes fire. This explosion of heat in turn causes even more kundalini to flow down.

Concrete concepts automatically wither and disappear. Rest in the feeling of utter satisfaction. You are touching reality, and at the same time you are experiencing bliss. Blissful energy explodes into an intense awareness of the wisdom of nonduality, and you touch an unprecedented level of universal reality.

You might even experience the white, red, or black visions that follow dissolution of the elements. This is a natural part of the process, so simply let go. Any vision that appears will help you to break down your concrete concepts. As more wind energy enters the central channel, your preconceptions will disappear. This is a naturally transcendent experience. Go beyond ego and self-pity. Touch totality.

Again, do the vase meditation. Bring the upper airs down and feel the energy and bliss at the navel chakra. Bring the lower energies up. The reaction is so strong that the inner fire explodes into flame. This time it blazes up beyond the heart chakra to reach the throat chakra, where it energizes great bliss. The blaze of the inner fire fills the throat chakra. The flame wraps itself around the *om* three times and superheats the throat chakra. Blissful kundalini drips down from the throat chakra through the heart chakra to the *short a*, causing the fire to blaze even more intensely.

Breathe in again. The inner fire explodes so strongly that it blazes up the central channel, passes through the heart and throat chakras, and reaches the crown chakra, where it energizes intense bliss and the clear light nature of nonduality.

The *ham* melts, and unimaginably blissful kundalini flows down to the throat. The throat chakra is filled with kundalini, the union of the white male and red female energies, and you experience incredible bliss. The blissful energy then flows down to the heart chakra, filling it. As the heart chakra fills, you unify the bliss with nonduality.

Finally the kundalini flows down to the *short a* at the navel. The inner fire explodes limitlessly and fills your entire Heruka body from the feet to the crown with blissful heat. The airs flow wherever the heat goes and send streams of kundalini throughout your entire body. You are utterly filled with bliss. Feel incredible pleasure, and unify it as much as you can with the wisdom of nonduality. Without intellectualizing, just be aware. Every movement of energy is helping your consciousness to unify with bliss and universal reality.

The intensity of the heat causes the airs to enter the central channel forcefully, thus energizing even greater heat and bliss. The more heat you generate, the more intense your response at the heart, throat, and crown chakras. This in turn causes more kundalini to flow down, which energizes even more bliss. Unimaginably blissful kundalini comes down. All the chakras are activated, but especially the navel chakra, where you are maintaining intense awareness of yourself as one with the *short a.*

❦ EXTRAORDINARY BLAZING AND DRIPPING

Focus your concentration on the *short a*; you are the *short a.* Again perform the vase breathing. Bring the air in, push down, and hold the upper airs at the navel chakra so that they meet and embrace the lower airs. They all absorb into the *short a* and activate incredible heat. An especially strong wind comes from the lower chakra, energizing it and activating the *short a.*

Even though the *short a* itself is very subtle, its heat is so strong that it activates the upper chakras. Much blissful nectar flows down from the heart so that the fire at the navel blazes and explodes into the central channel. The inner fire goes all the way to the heart chakra, filling it with the inner fire blaze. It explodes even more and goes to the throat chakra, filling it with the fire blaze. The crown chakra is also filled. Simultaneously the kundalini is flowing down, further intensifying the explosions of heat from the *short a.*

The inner fire blazes down from your navel chakra all the way to your feet. Your entire Heruka body is pervaded by the flames of the inner fire. All your chakras and channels are filled with the inner blaze. At the same time, you are totally one with the *short a.*

You see all the chakras with pristine clarity, as if you possess telepathic awareness. Because your entire deity body is one blazing inner fire and you are one with the inner fire, you can see the entire universal reality without any obstacles. Your intense bliss is aware of the wisdom of nonduality. Experience bliss throughout your entire body and have intense awareness of nonduality.

Next, visualize that from your brow chakra and your right nostril, the blazing inner fire flashes out like lightning into the universe. It reaches all the supreme beings, all the Buddhas and bodhisattvas of the ten directions, especially the great lineage lamas, Tilopa, Naropa, Marpa, Milarepa, Gampopa, and the great yogi Je Tsongkhapa.

The fire enters their bodies through their left nostrils, touches their four chakras, and melts their kundalini. This blissful energy emanates through their right nostrils and enters your body through your left nostril. All their supremely blissful kundalini energy comes to your crown, throat, heart, and navel chakras and generates great blissful inner heat. You experience utter bliss: blissful chakras, blissful channels, blissful everything.

Don't intellectualize. Just be aware of the experiences and let go. While contemplating the *short a,* perform the vase meditation and these four visualizations again and again.

We will now offer a dedication in accordance with our motivation at the beginning. "May all sentient beings discover blissful channels and chakras, and may the blissful winds enter the central channel. May they all discover the great blissful kundalini experience by developing inner fire in the central channel. May all sentient beings thereby achieve the totality of the illusory body and clear light wisdom."

18. Good Things and Bad Things Can Happen

⚜ DON'T INTELLECTUALIZE

Inner fire meditation is not something intellectual. No matter how much I talk to you about it, it is mere words until you experience inner heat for yourself. Just do the meditations and get the results. Your experiences will then guide you in the practice, so that you know what is dangerous and what is safe.

Don't force anything. As Lama Tsongkhapa explains, too much force can produce wind disorders, which involve interferences to the channels and winds. Do the vase breathing gently and contemplate the *short a*. Just be aware of what is happening, and let go. At a certain point the process will happen automatically.

You don't need to grasp or to intellectualize. Experience intense awareness of the *short a*, with no concern for past, present, or future, for right or wrong, for existence or nonexistence. Without intellectualizing, simply rest in the state of superawareness. Actually, inner fire meditation doesn't allow you to intellectualize. Of course, you have to use your intellect at the beginning in order to build up the inner fire, but you reach a point where you stop intellectual games. You simply let go, and let yourself experience it. It is then that you build the real inner fire.

The basic meditation is to contemplate and penetrate the *short a*, but in order to cause the winds to enter the central channel strongly, you need to engage in the technical inner fire meditations. In the beginning you might find them a little difficult, but eventually you won't need to apply any effort. You will be surprised to find that you are doing inner fire meditation effortlessly.

Whenever concentration, bliss, and clarity are strong, however, you do not need to use these technical meditations. At those times you simply let go and contemplate. When you reach the point where you can naturally and effortlessly hold the winds in strong vase meditation at the navel chakra, the airs will automatically produce blazing of the inner fire in the central channel. The magnetic pleasure will automatically be activated, kundalini will flow, and you will experience bliss not just in your channels and chakras but throughout your entire body. Every movement of the energies will be blissful. You won't have to apply pressure or do any special breathing. Everything will happen naturally. Continue your practice until you reach that point.

❧ INNER HEAT, ORDINARY HEAT

Correct inner fire meditation definitely produces heat. If you use these meditation techniques taught from the experience of Tibetan lamas, there is no doubt that inner heat will come. There is no way that the heat will not come.

The real inner heat gained through concentration melts the kundalini in the central channel, and this produces bliss, which is then used to understand nonduality. The unified bliss and wisdom of nonduality consumes superstitions and ego conflicts. We do not have bamboo, pine, or olive trees to burn as our inner fuel, but we do have plenty of ego garbage and superstitions. The main function of inner fire is to burn all our delusions and superstitions and allow a nonsuperstitious, simultaneously born great blissful wisdom to grow.

All nonconducive energy is burned by the inner fire, and only the useful energy remains. Our meditation causes tremendous energy to be absorbed into the central channel, which automatically draws in all the garbage from the other channels. Upon entering the central channel, this negative energy is transformed and perfected so that it can no longer harm you.

Lama Tsongkhapa explains that the real inner heat starts very gently; the heat is very small and very subtle, and it starts deep within the body. It is also heavy heat. Although the Tibetan word used to describe the quality of the heat translates literally as "heavy," it doesn't mean heavy in the ordinary sense. Rather, the heat should be gentle and should arise slowly and extensively. Inner fire should have the earth quality of strength, the fire quality of heat, the water quality of smoothness and softness, and the air quality of gentle movement.

Inner fire meditation should not only produce heat, however, but produce it in the right place. As I mentioned, real inner heat should arise from deep inside the body, and this happens when you visualize the *short a* more toward the spine. The bliss then also arises from deep inside the body. Tremendous heat that arises between the skin and the flesh, for example, is ordinary inner heat, and it is not what we want to produce. It is not useful. The skin can feel painful and burning to the touch. I experienced this many years ago when I first tried to practice inner fire. Going out in the sun for even a short time was unbelievably painful, like being in a fire or in boiling water.

Ordinary inner heat is transitory and unstable. It comes and goes, and it can flare up in various places. Between the skin and the flesh is just one example. Ordinary inner heat is very painful and uncomfortable, and it can cause sickness. The whole process can become dangerous when you practice incorrectly. Instead of feeling bliss, you end up feeling miserable. But don't be discouraged if you have a few bad experiences; at least you can learn from your mistakes.

In order to increase the inner heat, you can sometimes imagine that your entire body becomes the central channel. Inner fire then rises and pervades your whole body, from your crown to your feet. It is as if you are wearing clothes made of fire or as if you are in a tent of flames. Another technique is to imagine four suns, one in each of the cardinal directions, giving incredibly strong heat energy.

Also, His Holiness the Dalai Lama once told me that pressing a little just below the navel helps to increase bliss and heat. Even though doing this may cause you to lose your focus on the vase meditation to some extent, it helps you to generate bliss and heat. Touching below the navel when the inner heat is activated causes you to feel pleasure in your entire nervous system, especially in your crown chakra. The movement of inner heat is always linked to the crown chakra.

The bliss of inner fire begins at the secret chakra as well as at the navel chakra, but you should keep your attention on the navel chakra. Contemplating chakras other than the navel could bring heat and bliss more quickly, but this quick heat is not the proper inner heat. Concentrating at the navel chakra is best. On the other hand, in order to increase the blissful energy you can sometimes move the *short a* to the secret chakra and then do the vase meditation.

The main point, however, is to concentrate single-pointedly on the *short a* and develop stable inner fire in the central channel. This technique leads eventually to the experience of simultaneously born bliss.

❦ Bliss and Nonduality

Whenever heat begins, bliss begins. This is because of the power of the absorption of the winds, the power of the *short a*, the power of concentration, and the power of the melting of the drops within the central channel. You really taste the chocolate when all these factors are gathered together.

During inner fire meditation, it is important to recognize the blissful nature of any heat—in fact, of every physical and mental sensation—that arises. You should also recognize its nature of nonduality, clarity, radiance, transparency, and its reflection-like quality, so that the bliss itself becomes the wisdom of nonduality. Also, whenever you experience nonduality, you should recognize its blissful character.

As soon as we feel any bliss, we should put effort into generating the wisdom of nonduality. This is important from the very beginning. The bliss itself should be digested and transformed into wisdom. Bliss becomes wisdom, wisdom becomes bliss. Otherwise, the experience becomes one of ordinary pleasure, an explosion of emotional desire and superstition. If we constructively build up the unification of bliss and nonduality, there is no danger of this happening.

If you don't have a strong comprehension of the non-self-existence of the bliss, there is a danger of experiencing overwhelming desire when you are not meditating as well. Whenever you open your eyes, many objects will magnetically attract you because your desire is aroused. If inner fire meditation produces more and more desire, you will become nervous, frustrated, and stressed.

When we experience any pleasure, we normally grasp at it, and our mind becomes dark, overwhelmed, and uncontrolled. Our pleasure becomes an obstacle that blocks us, like a wall; it is so concrete that we cannot see beyond it.

This comes about because we do not understand the fundamental nondual nature of existence. Without this understanding, inner fire meditation can produce tremendous sensory energy. If we are not careful and do not channel the energy in the right way, inner fire can produce tremendous desire.

However, this does not mean that we should not have pleasure. We should have pleasure! We can have incredible pleasure, but it has to be controlled so that it can be transformed into clean-clear penetrative wisdom. It is good for human beings to experience pleasure, but it is wrong to experience it without wisdom. The unique quality of tantra is that it always unifies the male energy of bliss with the female energy of wisdom. These two must always occur together. We must put effort into ensuring this, because for so long this has not been our habit.

Remember, the right inner fire should bring the unification of bliss and the wisdom of nonduality. It is dangerous to forget this, because inner fire meditation is a very sensitive technique. Something will definitely happen, and if good things are not happening, bad things surely will.

☙ Uncontrolled kundalini

According to Lama Tsongkhapa, to melt the kundalini at the crown effectively, the inner fire must be ignited at both the navel and secret chakras and the winds must absorb into the central channel. This brings the yogi or yogini the experience of the four joys.

He points out that ordinary people, whose airs have not even entered the central channel, can also experience the melting of kundalini when the navel and secret chakras are energized. This is what causes ordinary orgasm. Some people experience this uncontrolled flow of kundalini during meditation. Simply by performing the vase breathing meditation, they experience blazing of the inner fire and melting of the kundalini. Blissful kundalini seems to come from everywhere, like falling rain. When this happens, there is danger of losing control of the kundalini energy. A man, for example, would lose semen.

Lama Tsongkhapa says that it is not desirable to have the kundalini flow uncontrollably. It is not correct to do inner fire meditation in the morning and have the kundalini flow spontaneously in the afternoon. There is a danger that it will merely increase ordinary physical desire.

Because kundalini is the main resource that we use in inner fire meditation, it is important for both males and females not to lose their sexual energy. Naturally, as beginners, we will find it difficult to control the energy when we experience it strongly; we have limited concentration and have not yet learned how to bring the airs into the central channel.

As Lama Tsongkhapa explains, it is not good to lose too much kundalini energy during meditation, but it is natural to lose a little occasionally. Don't panic and think, "Oh, I have lost some kunda-lini energy. Now I have broken my vows." When you are a beginner, you sometimes lose kundalini drops. Don't worry about it. I lose it some-times, and I don't worry about it.

Losing a small drop of liquid during your meditation causes no real damage or loss of strength. It does not make you unable to facil-itate the kundalini. However, experiencing orgasm through sexual contact or during sleep will cause loss of this facility and damage your strength. You can discover this through your own experience. When you lose kundalini energy strongly in meditation, the significant point is not that you are breaking your vow but that you are losing the strength of your kundalini. The physical exercises and concentra-tion will help you to develop control.

Control of kundalini energy is important even in ordinary orgasm. You cannot have a perfect orgasm if you cannot control your energy. It is the same in tantra. You cannot experience perfect bliss if you can-not control your energy. The fact is that if we lose our energy, we have no energy to utilize. In order to use energy, we need energy. If we don't have it, we cannot use it. This is logical, and you can see it clearly from your own experience. When you concentrate well and control your energy, you can experience more bliss, which you then unify with the wisdom of nonduality.

If kundalini starts to flow uncontrollably during your meditation and you begin to experience orgasm, try as much as possible to hold it and have it expand inside the secret chakra. Try to hold the energy there as long as possible. The longer you can hold it, the more pleasure you will experience and the more possibility you will have of utilizing that pleasure by unifying it with the universal reality of nonduality. In this way, you learn to control your body as well as your mind.

By the way, the semen that comes from the male sex organ during ordinary orgasm does not come from the central channel. For both males and females, the energy and bliss of ordinary sexual experience does not come from the central channel. You should be clear about this. The bliss of ordinary orgasm is produced by the kundalini touching the outside of the central channel.

In the logic of tantric yoga, if the kundalini energy generates such bliss when it touches the outside of the central channel, there is no question that it will generate incredible bliss when it flows inside the central channel. Bringing all the winds into the central channel gives rise to an experience of incomparable super-bliss.

Drawing the airs into the central channel and activating this bliss is mainly accomplished through the power of concentration. Therefore, someone who loses kundalini energy because they are living the normal life of a layperson can still be successful in the practice of inner heat yoga as long as they can maintain strong concentration during inner fire meditation. This is logical. Naturally, those who have weak concentration and also lose physical energy in this way will find it difficult to generate strong blissful energy.

Practitioners who experience uncontrolled leaking of kundalini before the airs have absorbed into the central channel must remember to bring the energy back up the channel before completely losing control. Lama Tsongkhapa points out that practitioners who lack strong concentration will find the kundalini more difficult to control the lower down it flows, especially if it flows below the navel chakra.

It is important to be aware of the point from which you must begin to reverse the flow of energy. Not only must this energy be brought back up, but it also must be spread throughout the nervous system. It can be dangerous and produce illness if it becomes blocked in any one place. Lama Tsongkhapa is giving this advice from his own experience, so you should try to understand clearly what he is saying.

The Kagyu tradition teaches many different techniques for reversing the downward flow of energy, but Lama Tsongkhapa mentions only one in *Having the Three Convictions*. Visualizing yourself as a deity, you sit in the full lotus position with your head bent a little forward. Your hands are placed together in vajra fists at your chest with the palms inwards and the index fingers stretched up to touch each other, thus forming a triangle. Your eyes are rolled upward. Gazing upward helps to draw the energy back up the central channel. The mind is not using the eye perception; it is contemplating the *haṃ* at the crown chakra.

Pull yourself strongly upward, even curling up your toes. Breathe in a little, focus on the *haṃ,* and repeat the syllable *hūṃ* twenty-one times. You feel that the energy is connected all the way down; you are aware of your secret chakra. As you say *hūṃ* over and over again, you feel the energy coming back up. You are concentrating strongly and you keep the lower muscles tight. Your body is as empty as a balloon, and you can direct the energy anywhere you want. You bring all the kundalini energy back up from the secret chakra and spread it at the navel, heart, throat, and crown chakras. From there, you spread it throughout the entire body.

Another technique is to visualize that the inner fire moves downward and pushes the kundalini back up in the same way that heat pushes up water when you boil it. Waves of blissful energy come to the heart chakra and spread throughout it. The blissful waves then continue up to the throat, crown, and brow chakras and spread through each of them in turn.

In his commentary on the completion stage of Chittamani Tara, the great yogi Je Pabongka explains the following meditation technique to help deal with uncontrolled kundalini. When the blissful, white nectar is melted by the inner fire and fills all the chakras down to the navel chakra, before it flows down into the secret chakra, visualize that it goes into the right and left channels and eventually fills all the channels of the entire nervous system. Je Pabongka explained this easy method in relation to Chittamani Tara practice, but we can also use it here.

❧

Sometimes during your inner fire meditation, the experience of bliss will cause your body to shake; this is related to movement of the air energies. You should not cultivate the idea that this has to happen. To have a restless body in the beginning is acceptable, but do not allow it to become a habit because it can be dangerous. Your mind reacts to the movement of the air, like a plane caught in turbulence; therefore, as long as the airs are moving, your mind will be distracted. The bliss of inner fire and the movement of kundalini energy should be gentle, blissful, peaceful, controlled, and subtle.

❧ Telepathic experiences

The Kalachakra Tantra speaks of the kundalini drops as having the potentiality of heaven and hell, of all the six realms. Inner fire meditation really shakes our entire nervous system and our entire view of reality. We don't want to have the energy of the lower realms inside our nervous system, as though it were sitting there waiting for us to die. We want to shake it up and bring it now to the navel chakra. When we do, we may suddenly see hell; we may suddenly be in hell.

Experiences of heaven and hell during meditation are possible because the entire universal energy is inside our subtle nervous system and can manifest from it. The lamas of all traditions agree that practitioners can suddenly see visions while doing inner fire meditation, as if they are dreaming. Such experiences are similar to telepathy, but they are not actual clairvoyance. You are moving in a dimension where there is telepathic energy, so you suddenly gain what seems like telepathic power. However, you still lack the attainment of single-pointed concentration, so don't become too excited. You have not yet gained clairvoyance.

Sometimes you may also be able to read other people's thoughts. Whether or not we call it telepathy, it is obvious that when you become more aware of the nature of your own mind, you will be more sensitive to the minds of other people. You will be able to read

the minds of others in accordance with your own level of development. This is nothing unusual. Again, don't believe that you have
actual telepathic powers simply because you have had a few good
experiences, and don't boast to anyone else about them. You should
control your mouth.

However, since the navel chakra is also known as the psychic
chakra, if you want to develop the telepathic power to read other people's minds, you should put effort into inner fire meditation. The
yogis of the past have stated that telepathic experiences will come.
They are not talking in this way just to attract our interest. However,
they also advise us to be careful when these telepathic experiences
start to happen.

You may see your entire nervous system as clearly as you see something on television. Or you may see different colors; each of the different air energies has its own characteristic color, so this is natural.[1]
The winds enter the central channel, you touch the awareness of nonduality, and such visions naturally arise.

You may experience the various visions that occur when the elements absorb, such as the appearance of a mirage, smoke, sparks, or
a dying candle. Sometimes you may see dakas and dakinis or pure
lands. You may even see the five Buddha families and think, "Wow,
the five Buddha families! Now I must have attained all their qualities!" Seeing these Buddhas in this way is possible.

These visions can be distracting, but stay calm. Remain aware of
them, but don't pay them any special attention. It is similar to meditating with a group of people. Although you don't pay any special
attention to the other people in the group, you are aware when
someone moves or does something. In the same way, maintain your
fundamental awareness of the *short a* and just relax about whatever
else happens.

It is possible to see incredible visions, both good and bad. Don't
become depressed when they seem bad. It is important to expect
interferences to your practice. Recognize even the bad ones as good,
in that they are signs that your meditation is effective. Do strong
purification practices and meditate intensively on emptiness, which is
the antidote to all interferences.

Many lamas mention that you may experience problems such as depression when you practice inner fire meditation. Lama Tsongkhapa does not mention this in *Having the Three Convictions*, but it is possible. You may expect inner fire meditation to bring only bliss, but difficulties do sometimes occur.

At times when your mind feels crowded and unhappy, this simple meditation might help. Breathe naturally. As you breathe out, feel that your mind becomes one with clear universal space. Concentrate on this clear universal space. This meditation can sometimes be useful.

❧ JUST LET GO

Surprising experiences can occur when you meditate on inner fire. Sometimes they are painful; sometimes they are super-blissful. It is a very sensitive technique.

For example, you may suddenly experience an explosion of incredible bliss. You might think, "Oh, this shouldn't be happening. I should be meditating on the *short a* instead of feeling blissful. I am being distracted by bliss. This is no good!" Or you may reach a certain point where you see a crystal-clear vision of reality. You might think, "What is this? I shouldn't be experiencing this. I should concentrate more on the *short a.*" You mustn't intellectualize like this.

Sometimes you might feel a primitive sensation, some awareness of concrete energy or a triangular shape, just below your navel. I'm just making some projections. Or you might reach a point where you experience a sort of numbness; you lose the clarity of your meditation and go into darkness. This is similar to one of the stages of energy absorption, which you can easily imagine because ordinary orgasm also brings the experience of energy absorption. Don't panic and think, "This is wrong. I should keep my meditation on inner fire." Just be calm. Maintain your fundamental awareness of the *short a,* and just let go when these different experiences happen.

At other times you may feel very pure and think, "Now I must be a bodhisattva on the first *bhumi.*" This is simply your imagination, not something real. When you have a good meditation, you may feel you are special, but don't overestimate. Practicing inner fire meditation with the thought that you are a great meditator undergoing powerful experiences is a symptom of ego. Many things happen when we meditate, so be careful. I worry about the human mind; we always have expectations, and our expectations are always a problem. We seldom manage to be reasonable.

Sometimes terrible feelings will arise, and you will think, "This is too much! I don't want to meditate any more." When inner fire meditation becomes a heavy burden, go back to the lam-rim and meditate on your precious human rebirth. When you check up, you will find that meditation is the best thing you can do with your life. In this way, lam-rim meditation supports your practice of the Six Yogas of Naropa.

If you experience the nonconceptual wisdom of nonduality, don't think, "But what about my inner fire meditation? What happened to my *short a* and my chakras?" Don't worry. Just let go. In your meditation you sometimes push the right button and experience a super-awareness of nonduality. If you worry about losing your meditation on inner fire, you will destroy the experience. Also, if incredibly blissful energy suddenly arises when you begin inner fire meditation, it is wrong to think, "Oh, no! I want red-hot inner fire. I don't want bliss."

You should unify whatever bliss arises with nonduality. However, the bliss can seem to shrink when you emphasize nonduality. Let's say that you are experiencing a certain amount of clear blissful energy, a ball of bliss. When you focus on nonduality, your ball of bliss becomes smaller, but that's okay. Just let go.

It is the same with the inner fire. Emphasizing its nonduality can cause the inner fire to become light and small rather than strong and concrete. As you continue to let go into nonduality, the fire becomes smaller and smaller, until eventually only a very subtle fire is left. At a certain point even this subtle fire might disappear. At that time, again place emphasis on bliss by means of the vase meditation or whatever technique you use to switch on the bliss. When you push the right button, the ball of bliss will balloon again.

When there is strong unity of the nuclear energy of bliss and nonduality, let go. Whatever blissful energy arises, let go. And when the energy of nonduality weakens, put more energy into nonduality. You will still have blissful energy, but it will be less and more subtle. Just let go.

Throughout the entire process, don't give up your fundamental penetrative awareness of the *short a*. And no matter what else happens, simply let go. Meditation is a state of being. You cannot have expectations. Each meditation is unique, a new experience. It is extremely important to let go in meditations such as inner fire. Intellectual cleverness does not work; it will only cause you to miss incredibly valuable experiences.

Our problem is that we often reject valuable experiences because we don't recognize their value. For example, when you experience bliss unified with emptiness and the *short a* disappears from your vision, you might think, "What is happening to my *short a*? Should I let it go or not?" Of course you should let it go! You need to be clean-clear about this. When you are experiencing such unified bliss, who cares if the *short a* disappears?

As I pointed out at the very beginning, inner fire meditation is fundamental. It is the foundation stone of all realizations. When you meditate on inner fire, you are using a secret key to open the door to all realizations. Listen to your subtle conscious experiences, and let go.

19. Simultaneously Born Great Blissful Wisdom

Success in inner fire meditation causes all the winds to first enter the central channel, then stabilize, and finally absorb there.

What is the sign that the air energies have entered the central channel? Normally, the passage of air is stronger through either the right or left nostril, alternating between the two. However, once the airs have entered the central channel, the breath moves equally through both nostrils. Lama Tsongkhapa says that even after gaining a constant signal that the energies have entered the central channel, we should continue the meditations until the process happens effortlessly.

However, even when our concentration is single-pointed and the airs enter the central channel effortlessly, we need to expand our experience until the airs have become stabilized and then totally absorbed in the central channel.

What is the sign that the airs have become stable? As the energies stabilize in the central channel, breathing becomes subtle and subdued, the movement of breath through the nostrils stops completely, and the abdomen ceases to move. This indicates that there is no movement of air in the two side channels.

At this point, in the Western medical view the yogi or yogini would be regarded as dead because breathing has stopped. But don't worry! We can take in air in many other ways, including through the pores of the body and the ears, for example. Western doctors may not know of these phenomena, but this organic breathing is a fact.

When yogis and yoginis gain control over their internal wind energies and can direct them into the central channel, they also develop control over the external wind energies. This is illustrated in the story I told you earlier about Lama Tsongkhapa going into meditation and extinguishing the fire from the butterlamps in the Lhasa temple. Tibetan lamas believe that the way in which Lama Tsongkhapa stopped the fire has great significance. If we are successful in inner fire meditation and learn to control our inner winds, we will also be able to put out fires with our meditation. And we will be able to go through solid matter, such as mountains.

The third phase in the process is absorption of the air energies in the central channel. By the time the winds have entered the central channel and stabilized there, our concentration and bliss would be very powerful. The energies then begin to absorb, and we experience the stages of dissolution that happen naturally at the time of death. With dissolution of the four elements, we experience the visions of a mirage, smoke, fireflies, and a flickering flame, followed by the white, red, and black visions, and finally the clear light. In this way we bring all the experiences of the death process into our life.

It is common for meditators to be afraid that they are dying when they first experience absorption of the energies. The sinking of the four elements has a negative connotation because it is normally followed by death, and we don't want anything to do with death, do we? But the yogi or yogini brings that experience into the here and now and transforms it into something blissful.

Absorption of the four elements and elimination of concrete, dualistic concepts brings an explosion of nonduality wisdom. This is not just some intellectual experience of emptiness. The sense perceptions have been knocked out and are no longer perceiving external objects. The yogi or yogini cannot physically move at all. The stronger their experience of the absorption of the airs, the more profound their comprehension of nonduality.

Finally, they go all the way through the white, red, and black visions and reach the subtlest mind of clear light. This is a natural process. Even during orgasm, there is experience to some extent of the three visions, and also of the clear light. The problem is that we are not aware of them. We do have such experiences, but we are def-

initely not using them in the right way. When we do use them correctly, we can produce the everlasting satisfaction of simultaneously
born great blissful wisdom.

🐚 THE FOUR JOYS

Our goal, our destination, is to experience simultaneously born bliss
and to unify it with wisdom. There are many degrees of bliss, but
what we want is the completion stage experience of bliss, in which the
winds have entered, stabilized, and utterly absorbed in the central
channel. The power of the inner fire and the force of the absorption
of the airs cause the kundalini at the crown to melt. It then flows
slowly down the central channel to the throat, heart, navel, and tip
secret chakras. Success in bringing the kundalini down the central
channel through these four chakras gives rise to the four joys. The
fourth joy is the experience of simultaneously born bliss.

This bliss is unique to tantra and cannot be developed without
the physical kundalini energy. Lama Tsongkhapa is clean-clear on this
point.

We first hear about the four blissful states of kundalini energy
during Highest Yoga Tantra initiations. They are joy, great joy, extraordinary joy, and simultaneously born joy. During initiation we only
imagine these four blissful states, but through inner fire meditation
we can actually experience them.

The entire process of generating the four joys begins with penetrative concentration on the *short a*. This activates the inner fire, which
causes the winds to enter, stabilize, and absorb in the central channel.
Lama Tsongkhapa says that the inner fire must be ignited at both the
navel and secret chakras. This causes the kundalini at the crown to
melt and flow slowly down the central channel. Lama Tsongkhapa
points out that the kundalini flow is naturally slow because of the
strength of the wind absorption. A prolonged flow of energy is what
we are seeking.

Your crown chakra is energized and your entire brain is blissful.
The kundalini flows like honey down to your throat chakra, and you
feel *joy*. The throat chakra is filled with bliss. Penetrate the throat

chakra, holding the energy there and feeling bliss unified with the wisdom of nonduality.

The kundalini then slowly flows from the throat to the syllable *hūṃ* at the heart chakra, where it activates *great joy*. Again, stay there, experiencing this special bliss and unifying it with wisdom.

Slowly the unified male and female energy of the kundalini flows down to the *short a* at the navel chakra, where it arouses *extraordinary joy*. With this blissful mind, meditate on emptiness. Feel that you touch the totality of universal reality.

From the blissful navel chakra, the energy flows down into the secret and middle secret chakras, filling them with blissful kundalini. Gradually it reaches the tip secret chakra and arouses *simultaneously born joy*. This fourth joy is the peak bliss, super-bliss. This simultaneously born bliss totally unifies with nonduality and actually becomes the wisdom of emptiness, the experience of clear light.

For a qualified practitioner, once the winds have entered, stabilized, and absorbed in the central channel and the kundalini has melted and come all the way down to the tip secret chakra, there is no way to lose the kundalini drops. Because the winds that normally move within the body have been absorbed, there is nothing to propel the kundalini out of the body.

It is important to understand Lama Tsongkhapa's thinking on this point. The yogi's or yogini's concentration, and therefore control, guarantees that the kundalini will flow properly. As the energy flows slowly down the central channel, it is definite that the profoundly blissful experience of the four joys will arise, culminating in the completion stage simultaneously born bliss when the kundalini reaches the tip secret chakra.

It is explained elsewhere that, with the four elements already absorbed, the white vision appears as the energy enters the secret chakra. The red vision appears when the kundalini reaches the middle secret chakra, and the black vision just before it reaches the tip secret chakra. Finally, the yogi or yogini experiences the totality of clear light when the energy enters the tip secret chakra.

After experiencing the four joys, you bring the energy all the way back up the central channel to experience the four joys of the reverse order. From the tip secret chakra you bring the energy through the jewel and secret chakras to energize the navel, heart, and then throat chakras. You meditate at each stage on the continually increasing bliss. Finally, the kundalini reaches your crown chakra and totally fills it with blissful energy. Your mind explodes with an intense awareness of nonduality, and you discover total satisfaction. The bliss experienced during this reverse process is even more intense than when the kundalini flows down.

❧ SIMULTANEOUSLY BORN GREAT BLISSFUL WISDOM

By now, the airs have entered, stabilized, and absorbed in the central channel, and the yogi and yogini have experienced the four joys. Because all the superstitions have ceased functioning, we can say that they are experiencing nonconceptual wisdom. But from the philosophical point of view, the state of clear light wisdom that they experience when they first begin to stop these superstitions is still conceptual because it does not yet totally embrace the essence of nonduality. It is as if there is thin silk between the meditator and reality. Therefore, after this initial experience of clear light, the yogi and yogini must practice until they have achieved the subtlest realization of clear light. Nevertheless, from another perspective, it could be said that they experience a nonconceptual mind because the eighty superstitions are cut at that time and they enter a state of complete peace.

This experience of simultaneously born bliss unified with the wisdom of emptiness is incomparable. The Sutrayana experience of the wisdom of emptiness cannot be compared with the experience of this subtle consciousness embracing nonduality. The gross mind is normally bound tightly by superstitions, so there is no space for the subtle mind to function. Inner fire meditation eliminates all gross concepts and awakens the very subtle clear light consciousness, which normally we do not touch, and this very subtle consciousness begins to function.

When you have reached a certain point of blissful awareness in this process, it is very important to let go. You have to stop intellectualizing and try to experience only penetrative awareness, without any conceptual thought. The Kagyupas, Nyingmapas, Sakyapas, and Gelugpas all agree on this point. The emphasis placed on developing the nonconceptual mind is the same in all traditions. This means that we should meditate on the fundamental nonduality nature of the mind.

The superficial, conventional, fantasy, dualistic mind is not the real nature of the human mind. Our fundamental nature is clean-clear, like crystal. We put our dualistic fantasies on top of this crystal, but these fantasies can never become one with our fundamental nature. Our real nature is always pure. This is powerful.

The totality of our fundamental nature does not have the relative appearance of face, arms, legs, and so forth. And there is no room within fundamental reality for the appearance of our self-pitying imagination; it automatically dissolves. Enlightenment, the total absence of self-pitying imagination, is the universal truth of all beings. So let go, be aware, and comprehend this fundamental nature.

At the same time, try to realize the Madhyamakan view of empti-ness: your legs are not you, your stomach is not you, your mind is not you. Don't think that you have no experience of emptiness. "I hardly even know the word 'emptiness,' let alone anything about how to meditate on it." To some extent, we all have the experience of clear light. We have it at death, for example; and we have all died many times already. You also experience it every day when you go to sleep; and you experience the clear light mind when you have an orgasm. At these times, the concrete concepts of the self-pity mind naturally break down. Not perceiving things as concrete is good enough to qualify as an experience of emptiness.

Experience intense superawareness of nonduality. Go into the zero of emotional objects, the zero of grasping objects, and the zero of unkindness objects. Touch this fundamental reality and feel truth. It is more real than your usual crowded, fanatical concepts. Let go, so that the space of zero is full of wisdom, full of love, and full of joy.

Catch the nonduality nature of the bliss, contemplate it, and let go. Do not let it be diverted into samsaric pleasure, if you want the right results to come. Let me try to explain. Suppose that you are attracted to Wonder Woman. She appears in front of you, and the attraction is there. Suddenly, she transforms into rainbow light in the space of blue sky. Desire disappears. Your entire relationship to her changes. She is there, but also not there. There is a new awareness.

In a similar way, when you recognize the bliss as the transparent, transcendental wisdom of nonduality, everything changes. This bliss is not concrete; it has the nature of rainbow light. Everything becomes light when you unify bliss with nonduality. Everything assumes a transcendental appearance and becomes as clean-clear as crystal.

If you have a strong orientation toward the Sutrayana way of understanding emptiness, the tantric way of actualizing emptiness could seem almost like a distraction or an interference. Sutrayana speaks of emptiness in quite different terms. It explains it with a negating approach, almost as a nihilistic experience. On the other hand, in tantra you try to have a strong vision of unity: everything becomes emptiness. However, there is no difference in the nature of emptiness as described in Sutrayana and Tantrayana. Emptiness itself is the same; but there is a big difference when it comes to the experience of emptiness.

Unifying bliss with an intense awareness of nonduality brings more light, more brightness, more clarity. The bliss itself is intense awareness, like lightning in the sky. This bliss is transparent, like a reflection, a rainbow, a crystal. A crystal is a good example for the experience of the unity of bliss and nonduality. The crystal itself exists while at the same time it reflects and contains other phenomena. Bliss also holds everything and reflects its nondual nature. The bliss itself becomes translucent, omnipresent wisdom energy embracing all universal phenomena. In other words, the bliss becomes wisdom; it becomes clear light embracing the entire universal reality.

This bliss is unique; it is a transcendental experience with no worldly concrete concepts of dualistic grasping. Ordinary pleasure usually increases our attachment, but the more we experience this bliss, the more content we become and the less we look outside. When you discover your own inner apple, you are not interested in looking for an apple anywhere else. Your mind is not distracted by external things. Because of your attraction to your inner apple, you have less dualistic superstition functioning to involve you in the external world. Psychologically you are satisfied.

When we have a blissful experience, we normally try to possess it; we don't let go. We think, "This is mine, not yours!" Actually, it is universal. You are experiencing something, but it is not even happening within the space of your own body. It is happening somewhere out there. The point I am trying to make is that you have the experience, but you yourself totally disappear. You experience it somewhere in space. This experience goes beyond your body, beyond your possession, beyond your normal circuit. This is very important to understand. The relative you disappears, as well as any impression of the relative sensory object you are experiencing. At the moment we are too involved with *my* body, *my* things, *my* heart chakra. All of these have to be dissolved into emptiness.

Basically, we have to unify bliss with nonduality. It is just an intellectual concept when I talk about it, but I want you to get some feeling for it. It takes time to discover the nonduality of bliss, to discover its non-self-existence and nonconcreteness. We need a lot of practice and a lot of experience. Words cannot convey an exact picture. Unifying bliss with the wisdom of nonduality is very profound, the most subtle and profound experience in the world.

Meditate until your mind reaches such states of bliss and nonduality. Eventually you will experience simultaneously born great blissful wisdom, which leads to Vajradharahood.

20. Becoming Vajradhara

❧ EMBRACING A CONSORT

According to Lama Tsongkhapa, meditators are qualified to practice with a consort when, through inner fire meditation, they have perfectly learned the three stages of entering, stabilizing, and absorbing the winds; and, through familiarity with this practice and the power of the absorption of the winds, they have developed complete control over the flow of kundalini and thus experienced simultaneously born bliss. In order to increase the experience of the four joys, the yogi or yogini can then practice with a consort.

The great yogi Je Pabongka, on the other hand, explains in his commentary on the completion stage of Chittamani Tara that the yogi or yogini can practice with a consort when the heart chakra opens and the kundalini flows. His view is that they should not practice with a consort until they have opened the tightness of the knots of the heart chakra. In other words, they are not qualified for the practice until the airs have not only absorbed in the central channel but begun to absorb at the heart chakra. To engage in the practice before this point is a mistaken action and a cause of rebirth in the lower realms.

Now, I would like to debate with Lama Tsongkhapa. Je Pabongka's view is that a yogi or yogini is ready to practice with a consort only when the winds have absorbed in the heart chakra and opened it by releasing the knots there. Lama Tsongkhapa, however, says that they can practice with a consort when the entering, stabilizing, and absorbing of the winds becomes a habitual experience and they can control the flow of kundalini.

I am not quite clear myself about these two statements. It seems to me that it is still possible that the heart chakra will not be open even though the airs have entered, stabilized, and absorbed in the central channel, as Lama Tsongkhapa explains. In this case, how can the practitioner be qualified to practice with a consort? Even though the energy has entered, stabilized, and absorbed in the central channel, it is possible that the yogi or yogini still does not understand emptiness and thus is not ready to practice with a consort. Think about this point.

Why is a consort necessary? At this point, the airs have already entered the central channel, stabilized, and absorbed. The four elements have ceased and the yogi or yogini has seen all the visions. With the flowing of the kundalini energy, they have experienced the four joys, culminating in the experience of simultaneously born bliss, and with that bliss they have comprehended nonduality. In other words, they have gone beyond grasping. Since they have already experienced simultaneously born great blissful wisdom, why do they need to practice with a consort?

The point is that there are degrees of these experiences: degrees of air absorption, degrees of bliss, and degrees of realization of nonduality. Practice with a consort causes the airs to enter the central channel more strongly; and the more strongly the airs enter, the more strongly they will stabilize and absorb, and the more bliss will be generated. The purpose of practicing with a consort is to increase these experiences, and eventually to energize total absorption of the winds at the heart chakra, total bliss, and total realization of nonduality. Up to this point, the yogi or yogini has used a mental consort in meditation and has only begun to open the heart chakra. They need the help of a daka or dakini to totally open it. To energize the complete experience of great bliss, the male and female must help each other to bring the embracing energy into the central channel.

There is a lot of confusion about consort practice, so you should understand clearly what Buddhist tantra has to say about it. The completion stage experience of great bliss achieved with a consort is incredible. It is beyond expression, beyond all concepts, beyond words. Accepting a consort is the unsurpassed way to achieve enlightenment. In fact, having reached the point of being qualified to take a consort, a yogi or yogini will definitely become enlightened in that life; they will achieve Vajradharahood.

It is also explained that both the male and female practitioners should be qualified to practice and should be of equal good fortune and intelligence.[1] When the male and female partners are equally qualified, they both experience the absorptions.

Je Pabongka also explains that the consort should be shown to you by your deity, your lama, or the dakinis. Of the four types of consorts, he considers the best to be the mantra-born consort, which means someone who has become qualified through their practice of tantra.[2]

Once the yogi or yogini has experienced bliss with a consort, each time they meditate on emptiness, they recollect the experience exactly and enter directly into blissful samadhi. This is not like our experience of eating mozzarella cheese: we eat it once and like it, but then we need to eat it again to get the pleasure. Without actually eating it, we don't get the satisfaction. However, for yogis and yoginis who have reached a certain level of development, it is enough for them to have the experience with a consort just once. Merely by remembering their previous experience with a relative consort, they will go effortlessly into deep samadhi and experience perfectly all the absorptions. Anyway, in the terminology of tantra, emptiness is the absolute consort, and finally that is enough.

❧ THE OTHER FIVE YOGAS

As I mentioned earlier, Lama Je Tsongkhapa lists the Six Yogas of Naropa as the yogas of inner fire meditation, the illusory body, clear light, transference of consciousness, transference into another body, and the intermediate state.

Lama Tsongkhapa explains that after practicing with a consort and deepening the realization of simultaneously born blissful wisdom, the yogi or yogini meditates on the waking-state practices of illusory body yoga and clear light yoga. These two subjects are derived from the Guhyasamaja Tantra.

People often misunderstand the term "illusory body," thinking that it merely refers to the practice of seeing everything as an illusion. Lama Tsongkhapa says that this is not the case. In fact, when the yogi or yogini arises from the experience of the totality of clear light, their very subtle wind instantaneously manifests as an illusory body. Resembling a deity, this body is known at this stage as the impure illusory body. It is subtle and delicate, is not composed of flesh and bones, and is separate from and does not depend upon the gross body. The practitioner can manifest this illusory body, perform many beneficial actions for others, and then return to their ordinary gross body. Method and wisdom are now unified; they occur simultaneously.

The yogi or yogini continues their practice in order to deepen their realization of clear light and to develop the pure illusory body, which is even more subtle than the one previously achieved.

In addition to meditating on clear light during the waking state, yogis and yoginis also practice the clear light of sleep; and during sleep they practice dream yoga meditation. Lama Tsongkhapa explains how dream yoga is gradually developed on the basis of meditation on the clear light of sleep. While going to sleep, you again meditate on the energy entering, stabilizing, and absorbing in the central channel. You experience the absorptions of the four elements, the three visions, and then reach the clear light experience.

Actually, this is a natural process. When we go to sleep, the absorptions of the elements and experience of clear light happen automatically. This sounds good, but right now our sleeping is an ignorant experience. Yogis and yoginis, however, train themselves to be conscious of the entire process. Having meditated successfully and held the clear light experience, they can easily move from there into dream yoga. We naturally manifest a dream body when we dream; yogis and yoginis, however, after experiencing the clear light of sleep manifest an illusory body.

As Lama Tsongkhapa points out, the practice of dream yoga is part of the illusory body yoga. In order to accomplish it, we need to be accomplished in meditation on the clear light of sleep; and in order to succeed in that, we need to have experienced the clear light in the waking state. First we learn to work with the clear light in our waking state, and then in our sleep. After that we can succeed in dream yoga. However, success in both waking- and sleeping-state yogas depends upon inner fire meditation. Inner fire is the fundamental practice.

Once we have attained proficiency in the illusory body of the dream state we can succeed in intermediate state yoga. Hence this also depends on the power of inner fire meditation. The same applies to the yoga of the transference of consciousness and the yoga for projection of consciousness into another body. These two also depend upon the ability to direct the energies into the central channel. Without the preliminary of the winds entering the central channel, these two yogas of transference of consciousness cannot happen.

Some people think that transference of consciousness is easy, but Lama Tsongkhapa disagrees. He states clearly that you must first practice inner fire meditation and be able to direct the energies into the central channel before you can practice transference of consciousness. Lama Tsongkhapa is not only giving his own opinion on the matter. In his commentary on transference of consciousness, he quotes the words of Shakyamuni Buddha extensively and transmits the lineage perfectly. According to Lama Tsongkhapa, transference of consciousness is not an easy task.

All these subjects need to be studied in detail when the time comes to practice them, so it is not necessary to elaborate on them now. Remember that inner fire is the practice fundamental to all of them. It is like a chain linking you to all the realizations. Understanding this is in itself a profound realization.

Lama Tsongkhapa's special field is tantra, and he is especially renowned for his teachings on the illusory body. His way of describing the entire process, complete with meditation instructions, is distinctive and incredibly clear. His teachings are very helpful and inspiring. While giving this teaching, I have been feeling especially grateful to Lama Je Tsongkhapa. His profound explanations of the Six Yogas of Naropa have inspired me to feel much devotion for him. There is no doubt in my mind that he was a great mahasiddha.

Earlier in the text, Lama Tsongkhapa quoted Marpa as saying that he had received the heritage of these teachings from "the gatekeeper of Nalanda," which means Naropa. In ancient times, the large monasteries were surrounded by walls with a gate in each of the four cardinal directions. At each gate sat a pandit, whose task it was to give teachings or to debate with anyone who wanted to do so.

Marpa also states that he received the techniques of the nine mixings, transference of consciousness, inner fire meditation, and consort practice in accordance with the Hevajra Tantra. He continues, "By means of inner fire, I actualized the four joys; and by means of consort practice, I developed them to completion."

In order to develop ourselves and benefit others, we too need to receive all these methods just as Marpa did. Let's pray for this to happen. "May we all develop indestructible samadhi meditation on the *short a* and thus discover great blissful chakras, great blissful energies, and great blissful kundalini. May we develop the true inner heat, and thereby experience the blissful states of the four joys. May the bliss itself become intense penetrative awareness of the wisdom of nonduality. In this life, may we all attain the union of the illusory body and clear light, thereby becoming Vajradhara."

PART SIX

Living with Inner Fire

21. Your Pleasure Is Your Responsibility

By now, you should have all the information you need on the subject of inner fire. Practice the various meditation techniques as much as possible. If you use these techniques, your spiritual growth is ensured because you will gain the strength and energy to practice continuously. You need the reinforcement of positive experiences, but it is not good to experience a little success and then stop the practice. Lama Tsongkhapa points out that it is important to continue the practice once you have some signs of progress.

It is said that it is possible to attain enlightenment in a few years, or even a year, by means of practicing inner fire meditation. It is such a true method that if you practice it sincerely, the discovery of totality is not far away.

Anyone with enough intelligence and good fortune can experience the results of inner fire simply by meditating on these techniques as instructed, even if they do not believe in them in a religious way. This makes them especially appropriate for Westerners, who are generally not orientated toward religious belief. Inner fire meditation is scientific and logical, and you can experience its results without having to wait for a future life. You don't even have to believe in future lives. You just have to do the practice. In any case, maybe it is better to believe that you will be enlightened in this life through practicing the Six Yogas of Naropa than to believe in future lives.

I want you to have a strong, powerful motivation. Buddhism considers mental attitude to be fundamental to the way we interpret our life and our world, so it is important to have the correct motivation for our practice. Motivation is the way to remain interested and clear, because it helps us to see which way to go.

Motivate strongly, pray strongly, to experience inner heat, blissful channels, blissful winds, blissful kundalini, and the union of simultaneously born bliss and wisdom. Be brave! Think, "Why can't I do what Milarepa and Lama Tsongkhapa did?" Then resolve, "I have no choice—I must practice inner fire meditation!"

JUDGING BY YOUR OWN EXPERIENCE

Try as much as possible to actualize nonconceptual, indestructible samadhi and the union of bliss and emptiness. Don't think, "I am not very accomplished in evolutionary stage yoga, so I should not practice completion stage." Lama Tsongkhapa himself did four sessions of meditation every day. He practiced evolutionary stage yoga in the morning and completion stage yoga in the afternoon. Practicing the two together is the right thing to do.

Inner fire meditation can actually help you to realize evolutionary stage yoga. Initially, you might find concentrating on the deity and attaining samadhi difficult; but when you start to practice inner fire—*pam!*—everything comes together. Also, the Tibetan tradition usually explains a graduated path to the attainment of realizations: first you do this, and then you do that. Inner fire meditation helps this process and this graduated process helps inner fire meditation.

Also, you shouldn't think, "How can I meditate? First I should study for twenty or thirty years, and maybe then it will be reasonable for me to meditate. At present I am ignorant of all the vast subjects of Buddhism; therefore, I could not possibly get even a glimpse of single-pointed concentration. In any case, I have a job and I'm very busy. How can I possibly try to develop samadhi meditation? Tibetan monks who live in the mountains and never see anybody can develop single-pointed concentration, but I am always surrounded by crowds of people. It is impossible for me to meditate."

This thinking is definitely wrong. We are always making excuses. You should do your meditation every day, and at the same time, you can work, recite prayers, and perform other activities. It is possible to engage in other activities while developing single-pointed concentration, especially once you have received instructions on inner fire. Most lamas of Je Tsongkhapa's tradition combine study and meditation all their lives. They meditate on a concentration object every day as well as do other activities.

As beginners, we have to try to bring the experience of heat and bliss to the chakras and channels and thus achieve clear light. Even though we have not yet reached the clear light stage, we have already had some experience of it. Clear light is fundamentally existent within us. We have to expand this experience until we reach totality. This is not something to merely talk about intellectually. You have to judge when you need gas and how much you need. If you turn the gas too high, you will overcook: you will become overblissful and overheated. It'll be a disaster! So judge carefully.

In Shakyamuni Buddha's approach to human growth, you are the one responsible. Buddha or the guru or God is not responsible. You have to judge by your own experience, which is why you need to develop confidence in yourself. Remember the story of Milarepa. After he had spent a couple of years with Marpa, Marpa sent him away. Milarepa was then alone in the mountains with no one he could ask for advice. He was empty-handed; he had nothing.

You can definitely judge for yourself. You should appreciate this and believe in yourself. You know which technical meditations you need and when to apply them. Sometimes you won't need any of the techniques. Just with natural, subtle breathing, your concentration will be reasonably good, your inner fire energy will grow, and you will feel blissful. In that state of mind, you will have no superstition, no pressure of mundane thoughts. It will be a clean-clear state, with no this or that and with no movement toward sensory objects. You learn to let go of many things.

Also, just as you change your friends, you can change the statues and pictures of Buddhas and lamas on your altar. Don't think that you must have a particular picture on your altar because otherwise other people will think that you are not being respectful. Who cares about what other people think? This is just politics. When you pay attention to such criticism, you are not communicating with yourself. It is your business, not theirs. It is your altar, and arranging it is your experience. Put Mickey Mouse on your altar if you find it helpful. Use whatever communicates with you and helps you to grow.

175

For example, when you are grasping, dissatisfied, and over-whelmed by desire, place an image of the fasting Buddha on your altar, and look at it. Or put a skeleton there. Get a human bone, put it on your altar, and look at it. It might give you a more powerful message than you are getting from a photo of your lama. You are not abandoning the Buddhist religion by not placing an image of Buddha on your altar. Don't worry about what other people say. If something has meaning for you, just use it. You can change your altar whenever you wish. This month you can have the fasting Buddha; next month you can have something else. At this time I have an image of Lama Je Tsongkhapa on my altar because I am feeling especially close to him. I feel much devotion for Lama Tsongkhapa.

❧ YOUR PLEASURE IS YOUR RESPONSIBILITY

According to Lama Je Tsongkhapa, successful inner fire meditation brings physical as well as mental health because it increases the kundalini energy, which develops bodily strength. And the stronger your kundalini energy becomes, the greater the success you will have with inner fire meditation.

Taking care of your body is important because it is the source of simultaneously born bliss. For example, in order to increase the sexual energy of male-female kundalini, you should eat food that is high in protein and exercise regularly. It is logical that the more energy you have, the more you can use.

During periods of intensive practice of inner fire meditation, even laypeople should try to control the loss of sexual energy. According to Buddhist tantra, losing sexual energy during intercourse weakens the physical strength of your body. This weakening of the body then weakens the flow of kundalini. You do not have to believe this simply because it is what the Tibetan texts and Tibetan lamas say. Check your own experience.

This does not necessarily mean that laypeople should live like monks or nuns. However, when you are practicing strongly, you should control yourself and not lose kundalini. When you are not practicing strongly, there is no commitment not to lose energy; you just act normally.

Laypeople with a regular sex life should use the force of inner fire meditation to hold the kundalini in the secret chakra for as long as possible during intercourse. Imagine that you experience simultaneously born great blissful wisdom before you release the energy. Having this control brings even greater bliss and satisfaction, especially when you have generated strong energy within you because of your magnetic attraction to the other person. You can utilize this energy in the secret path to liberation.

Why am I telling you this? I don't want to ruin my reputation by having people say, "Don't go near Lama Yeshe! He burned out my married life and ruined my relationship." Tantra is very practical in emphasizing the use of desire energy. Of course, when we first meet someone we arouse pleasure and excitement within each other, almost to the point of energizing kundalini. Later all we do is energize misery! Instead of becoming each other's pleasure object, we become each other's prisoner.

Each of the four classes of tantra is meant for a particular type of practitioner. What differentiates one class of tantra from another is the intensity of the desire energy used in the path to enlightenment. In Action Tantra, great bliss is aroused by simply looking at all the beautiful deities; in Performance Tantra, smiling and laughing is used to energize bliss; in Yoga Tantra, blissful energy is generated from holding hands; and in Highest Yoga Tantra, the energy of the sexual embrace is used.

Having the Three Convictions states that lay practitioners even at the level of evolutionary yoga can rely upon a partner to some extent to develop bliss and wisdom. This practice is not exclusive to highly attained tantric practitioners. As long as you use this energy to generate the wisdom of nonduality, you can do whatever you want to do. This makes sense. As long as we are developing bright universal wisdom, it doesn't matter what tools we use. As long as you are clear that you are responsible for the growth of the totality of the simultaneously born great blissful wisdom of your own Vajradharahood, anything you do that benefits your growth is good, even if it is socially unacceptable. In any case, society has a dualistic structure, and its philosophies can make you more confused.

You are responsible for your own growth. As long as you are not harming yourself, turning yourself into a psychological or physical disaster, and are not harming any other sentient being, who cares what you do? The Buddhist attitude is that you take care of your own karma; you take care of your own baby. What society or anyone else says you should do is not important. What you do is your responsibility. Your pleasure is your responsibility.

On the other hand, don't think that happiness always comes from touching something outside yourself and never from inside. Happiness comes from inside you, so remember that you don't always need to play in your relationships.

You have to be very strong and straight with yourself. The reason I am saying this is that tantric practice can produce confusion in your life, and I want you to be clean-clear. Also, even though we may not agree with society's standards, we must not harm other people in our society. We have to have hearts big enough to accept the ideas of all kinds of people.

Let's dedicate the merit. "For the rest of our lives, may we grow in strength and apply great effort to gain success in inner fire meditation. We can then share our success so that the universal community attains bliss."

22. Never Forget Inner Fire

The yoga of inner fire is a profound teaching, and it should be used in a meaningful way. You should meditate on inner fire as much as possible. It is really such a simple technique.

It is good to set up a place for meditation wherever you are living. For a few dollars you can make a meditation box like meditators used in ancient times. Since you cannot lie down in a meditation box, at least while you are in it you have to sit up and meditate. It is good psychology to set yourself up in this way.

Be mindful of your experiences and keep a written record of them if you like. You have to understand that these technical meditations are set up in such a way that you will achieve results. Everybody who practices them should have some experiences.

We should practice as seriously as Naropa did. The Six Yogas of Naropa is a completion stage tantric practice that is both complete and profound. These six subjects contain the nucleus of the practices of both the father and mother tantras. The way to take the essence of these teachings is not through an intellectual approach but through action. You simply have to act. You must practice continuously.

When you practice inner fire in retreat, start by doing five or six short sessions each day. In the beginning it is better to do short sessions of perhaps an hour and a half each, because then you will do them well. When you become more accomplished, you can do sessions of many hours in length; if you do long sessions at the beginning, you will merely become sluggish and sleepy. Also, do the physical exercises for half an hour at least once a day.

When you are not in retreat, it is best to do the hatha yoga and the inner fire meditations early in the morning on an empty stomach. Also, since fire energy is naturally strong in the evening, this is a good time to meditate on inner fire, but only if your stomach is empty. People in the West tend to eat a large meal in the evening, so in that case it is better to do the practice in the morning.

All the inner fire meditations should be done with single-pointed concentration. This includes the meditations on melting the blissful kundalini energy; the entering, stabilizing, and absorbing of the winds; and the whole process of the sinking of the four elements and the arising of the three visions. They are all intended to be samadhi experiences.

People may feel some conflict between doing strong samadhi meditation and their daily meditation commitments. In the Tibetan system, you have permission to reduce your other prayers when you are doing strong single-pointed meditation, such as in an intensive retreat on inner fire. Your practice is the best prayer in any case. You can relax about relative prayers because you are doing absolute prayer. There should not really be any conflict. The most important point is the meditation. On the other hand, you shouldn't casually think, "I'm doing absolute prayer, so I can give up relative prayer." To rationalize like this can be dangerous. You have to think carefully about how to adjust your life.

During periods of intensive inner fire meditation, you should not sit too close to fires or get sunburned, as this may stimulate the wrong energies. It doesn't matter when you are not meditating intensively; at those times you can go to the beach as usual and burn yourself to a brown color.

Unfortunately, you should also avoid cold foods, such as ice cream. Eating very cold things damages your natural resource for inner fire meditation. Also avoid salty foods and drinks when you are doing inner fire meditation. You may think that Tibetans have no idea about chemicals and such things, but we have known about them for many hundreds of years. Also, you should not eat acidic foods, such as lemons. Many juices are said to be free of acid, but I have discovered that most of them are acidic. Avoid fish, too.

Inner fire meditators are also advised to wear light clothing. We should follow the middle way; our clothes should not be heavy and we should not be completely naked. It is especially important not to go naked in the sun because the hot rays can cause discomfort. Also, don't sleep under heavy blankets or thick feather quilts such as those used in Germany. Tibetan yogis advise that you shouldn't allow your body to get too hot. You should also not lift heavy weights or breathe forcefully, as you do when you blow up a balloon, for example.

Until your inner fire practice is stable, you should not expose yourself to confused situations. Conserve your energy a little. With inner fire meditation, you become extremely sensitive, so you must be conscious of what you are doing.

The most important point is to try to experience inner heat and bliss and then to unify your blissful experience with the wisdom of nonduality. You will eventually reach a point in inner fire practice when the mere movement of your breath will energize bliss and bring you physical and mental satisfaction.

The more bliss you feel, the more nonsuperstitious wisdom you should try to experience. This is why you need the energy generated from the various technical meditations. Concentration, bliss, and clarity will be weak when your kundalini energy is weak; therefore, you use these meditations to build up the energy. When the energy is strong, however, you don't need the meditation techniques. You stop intellectualizing and simply let go and contemplate. No matter how much I talk, it is just words. This is something you have to experience for yourself, and when you gain some worthwhile experience, you can share it with others. Just by being yourself, you will share with others.

You should cultivate bliss and nonduality not only during meditation sessions but in the breaks between sessions as well. You can bring inner fire into all your daily activities; use every experience of ordinary pleasure—every pizza and chocolate experience—to contemplate with intense awareness the inner fire in the central channel. When you are walking and talking, bring along inner fire. Take it with you when you go to the beach or to the mountains. When you touch water, feel it is blissful; when you see a fire, imagine that it is the inner fire; when you see light, imagine that it is kundalini energy.

When you experience blissful forms, colors, sounds, smells, tastes, and touch sensations, think that this ordinary pleasure adds petrol to the inner fire, causing it to blaze. Direct all the blissful energy into the inner fire in the central channel at the navel chakra. Tantra is very practical when it talks about taking desire and samsaric pleasure into the path to enlightenment.

The purpose of inner fire meditation is to increase pleasure. The yogi or yogini is simply saying, "I am not satisfied with the pleasure I already have. I want more. That is why I am practicing inner fire." However, you must never forget to unify the father aspect of bliss with the mother aspect of nonduality. In this way, your bliss helps the growth of your wisdom. For this reason, the tantric teachings tell us not to reject pleasure, but rather to utilize it. If you do not use it in this way, it becomes poison. Every experience that facilitates pleasure becomes the petrol to fuel your inner fire, and you unify that pleasure energy with the wisdom of nonduality.

All of us are trying our best to be completely happy. Houses, cars, refrigerators—we buy everything in the hope of making ourselves happy, but there is always something missing. Either the father bliss or the mother wisdom is missing. Look objectively at most people's lives. They may be intelligent and be making a lot of money in some high-powered business, but they do not seem to know how to put even ordinary bliss and wisdom together in their lives.

Tantra unifies these two, the father bliss and mother wisdom, and brings them together simultaneously. This is why Lama Tsongkhapa talked earlier about the unity of relative and absolute when he discussed the fundamental characteristics of the mind. In order to taste inner fire we have to understand the unification of the relative and absolute. We have to know how to put bliss and wisdom together. Inner fire meditation is a process in which we learn to unify bliss and emptiness inseparably. Bliss energy is emptiness; emptiness is bliss.

In the West we see so many people who are intelligent but have no bliss. They seem really disturbed. They can do many technical things, but their knowledge is dry and intellectual, so they find no satisfaction. Others with little intellectual knowledge but with perhaps a more practical approach to life find more satisfaction. Tantra tries to bring the intellect into actual experience and to unify it with blissful energy. When you can do this, you can eradicate all your worldly problems, all your pleasure problems.

Remember, every moment of our lives can become meditation. When you are awake, everything is meditation; when you sleep, everything is meditation; when you die, everything is meditation. Hearing this, you might think, "Wow! Fantastic! Let's make a movie about it." But it is true. Tantra is very profound.

I hope that you can gain some experience of the inner fire meditations. The most important thing is that you really touch something inside yourself. If this happens, I have absolutely no doubt that some transformation will take place. The beauty of inner fire is that you don't have to believe in anything for it to work. Just do the technical meditations and let go. The experiences and realizations will automatically come.

Don't forget that completion stage tantric meditations such as these can also help to bring Sutrayana realizations. For example, inner fire meditation can loosen attachment and help the bodhicitta mind to grow. Some people find that even though they have little experience of the preliminary practices, they can still achieve completion stage experiences.

I am very happy to have come here to my center and given teachings, and even though most of what I explained is just empty words, I tried my best to communicate with you in a reasonable way. In the twentieth century we all have such busy lives, so we are lucky to have had this chance to study Lama Je Tsongkhapa's teachings. And I feel lucky to see that you have tried to meditate. That is important for my mind. We have had only a short time to meditate, to experience, but we all tried our best, so my heart is happy. And I don't care that we only covered about twenty pages of Lama Tsongkhapa's commentary.

If I am alive and you are alive, perhaps we will see each other again. The next time we will discuss in detail the illusory body, the dream experience, the clear light experience, transference of consciousness, and consciousness going into another body. These subjects are more profound and sophisticated. You should work on what we have already covered, and we will pray that at some time in the future we will do the rest of the Six Yogas of Naropa. If we cannot do them next year, we can do them next life. Actually, I will pray that you receive these teachings from a realized teacher and not from a Mickey Mouse teacher like me.

I hope I didn't cause too much confusion. If you have some difficulty with your meditations or with the teachings, please don't hesitate to write to me. I have received this teaching a couple of times, but I am a lazy student, so I can make mistakes. If I did make mistakes, you should tell me. It is good to send me your questions—in that way, I learn too. I have time; don't think I don't have time. It is important that we work together. Don't think that I just come here, say a whole lot of confusing blah, blah, blah, and then leave you alone with your confusion. It is not true. I am not the most highly realized man, but I am a dedicated one. Maybe I am fooling myself, but I do have a wish to dedicate my life to others as much as possible. Even though I am a pretty simple monk, you should feel that I am with you—it is important.

We have been doing something so worthwhile together, so we should communicate with each other. It's not good to visualize Lama as God or something like that. We just need person-to-person communication. We can do this in a simple way: "Hello, how are you? I hope your heart is all right. I hope your nose is all right." Do you understand?

Thank you so much for your cooperation and discipline; discipline is important. And I am very happy with the quality of your loving-kindness and sincerity. You have integrated a rich inner quality with a rich outer quality, so I think you have been successful. Thank you so much. I dedicate all your energy—but even if we don't dedicate, karma will take care. It is good to have an attitude of dedication to others, of wanting to give to others. I am satisfied with what you are doing, and you should continue. Share your love, your wisdom, and your wealth and serve each other as much as possible. Live in harmony with one another and be an example of peace, love, compassion, and wisdom.

Try to be happy in your practice, to be satisfied with your life. Be reasonable in the way you grow, and don't ever think that it is too late. And don't be afraid of death. As long as you feel you have gained some experience, even death is no big deal. Life has been enjoyed. Even if you are going to die tomorrow, at least for today keep yourself straight and clean-clear, and be a happy human being. Because we are trying to bring reasonable satisfaction and reasonable joy into our lives, and to go reasonably beyond fear, it is most important that we meditate. When you accomplish inner fire, you will be satisfied, and you will also benefit others.

Milarepa, for example, mainly practiced. He did not teach much in his life; he meditated. I'm sure that Milarepa had his practice commitments, but when he went to the mountains he had no books with him. His commitment was in his heart. At a certain point you go beyond prayers, beyond words. Inner fire meditation is not for beginners who play with words and prayers. With inner fire meditation, ritual is not so important; what is most important is to concentrate and penetrate. This is the point. Milarepa is a perfect example. He was successful; he achieved bliss. Pray to be like Milarepa, like Lama Je Tsongkhapa. They did a good job; we should do a good job too.

"May we never forget the *short a* through all the ups and downs of the rest of our life. May we all achieve the realizations of the yogas of inner fire, illusory body, and clear light, just as Milarepa and Lama Tsongkhapa did, in order to benefit all the precious, suffering mother sentient beings."

Sanskrit Pronunciation Guide

For those unfamiliar with the way that Sanskrit words are rendered into English, the chart below offers an easy way to approximate the pronunciation of the Sanskrit terms in this book. For more precise instructions, please see Michael Coulson's *Teach Yourself Sanskrit* (Kent: Hodder and Stoughton, 1992).

Approximate English Equivalents of Sanskrit Sounds

SANSKRIT	ENGLISH
a	'but'
ā	'father'
i	'fit'
ī	'see'
u	'who'
ū	'boo'
ṛ and ṝ	'crust'
ḷ and ḹ	'slip'
ṃ	'mom'
ṅ	'ring'
c and ch	'chain'
ṭ, ṭh, t, and th	'top'
ḍ	'do'
ṇ	'no'
ś and ṣ	'she'

Table of Foreign Word Transliterations

Akshobhya	Akṣobhya
Amitabha	Amitābha
Amogasiddhi	Amoghasiddhi
arhat	arhat
Asanga	Asaṅga
Atisha	Atiśa
bhumi	bhūmi
bodhicitta	bodhicitta
bodhisattva	bodhisattva
Buddha	Buddha
Buddhadharma	Buddhadharma
chakra	cakra
Chakrasamvara	Cakrasaṃvara
Chandrakirti	Candrakīrti
Charya Tantra	caryā-tantra
Chittamani Tara	Cittamaṇi-Tārā
Chittamatrin	cittamātrin
Chittamatra	cittamātra
daka	ḍāka
dakini	ḍākiṇī
Dharma	Dharma
dharmakaya	dharmakāya
Ghantapa	Ghaṇṭapa
Ghantapada	Ghaṇṭapada
Guhyasamaja	Guhyasamāja
guru	guru
guru yoga	guruyoga
hatha yoga	haṭhayoga
Heruka	Heruka
Heruka Chakrasamvara	Heruka-Cakrasaṃvara
Heruka Vajrasattva	Heruka-Vajrasattva
Hevajra	Hevajra
Highest Yoga Tantra	anuttarayogatantra
Hinayana	Hīnayāna
karma	karma
kayas, the three	trikāya
Kriya Tantra	kriyā-tantra

kundalini	kuṇḍalinī
Luhipa	Lūipā
Madhyamaka	Madhyamaka
Maha-anuttara Yoga Tantra	mahānuttarayogatantra
mahamudra	mahāmudrā
mahapandit	mahāpaṇḍita
mahasiddha	mahāsiddha
Mahasiddha Naropa	Mahāsiddha Nāropa/Nāḍopa
Mahayana	Mahāyāna
Maitreya	Maitreya
Maitri	Maitrī
Maitripa	Maitrīpa
mandala	maṇḍala
Manjushila	Mañjuśīla
Manjushri	Mañjuśrī
mantra	mantra
Mantrayana	mantrayāna
mudra	mudrā
nada	nāḍa
Nagarjuna	Nāgārjuna
Nalanda	Nālandā
Naropa	Nāropa/Nāḍopa
nirmanakaya	nirmāṇakāya
nirvana	nirvāṇa
Padmasambhava	Padmasambhava
pandit	paṇḍita
Pandit Naropa	Paṇḍita Nāropa/Nāḍopa
Paramitayana	pāramitāyāna
Prasangika-Madhyamaka	Prāsaṅgika-Madhyamaka
Ratnasambhava	Ratnasaṃbhava
rupakaya	rūpakāya
sadhana	sādhana
sadhu	sādhu
samadhi	samādhi
samaya	samaya
Samayavajra	Samayavajra
sambhogakaya	saṃbhogakāya
samsara	saṃsāra
Saraha	Sāraha
Sautrantika	Sautrāntika
Shakya	Śākya
Shakyamuni Buddha	Śākyamuni Buddha
Shantideva	Śāntideva
shunyata	śūnyatā

siddha	siddha
Sutrayana	sūtrayāna
sutra	sūtra
Svatantrika-Madhyamaka	Svātantrika-Madhyamaka
tantra	tantra
Tantrayana	tantrayāna
Tara	Tārā
Tilopa	Tilopa
Tushita	Tuṣita
Vaibhashika	Vaibhāṣika
Vairochana	Vairocana
vajra	vajra
vajra body	vajrakāya
Vajrabhairava	Vajrabhairava
Vajradhara	Vajradhara
Vajradharahood	vajradharatā
Vajrasattva	Vajrasattva
Vajravarahi	Vajravārāhī
Vajrayana	Vajrayāna
Vajrayogini	Vajrayoginī
Vasubandhu	Vasubandhu
Yamantaka	Yamāntaka
yogi	yogin
yogini	yoginī

TIBETAN

bardo	bar do
Baso Chögyen	ba so chos rgyan
Butön (Rinchen Drup)	bu ston rin chen grub
Chökyi Dorje	chos kyi rdo rje
Damchö Gyeltsen	dam chos rgyal mtshan
den	ldan
Dorje Khadro	rdo rje mkha' 'gro
Dragpa Wangchug	grags pa dbang phyugs
Drigungpa	'bri gung pa
Drilbupa	dril bu pa (Skt. Ghaṇṭapa)
Dromtönpa	'brom ston pa
Gampopa	sgam po pa
Ganden	dga' ldan
Ganden Tripa	dga' ldan khri pa
Gelug(pa)	dge lugs (pa)
Gen	rgan
Gen Jampa Wangdu	rgan byams pa dbang 'dus

Geshe Jampa Tegchog	dge bshes byams pa theg mchog
Geshe Lama Könchog	dge bshes bla ma dkon mchog
Geshe Lobsang Donyo	dge bshes blo bzang don yod
Geshe Ngawang Gendun	dge bshes ngag dbang dge 'dun
Geshe Norbu Dorje	dge bshes nor bu rdo rje
Geshe Sopa Rinpoche	dge bshes bzod pa rinpoche
Geshe Tashi Tsering	dge bshes bkra shis tshe ring
Geshe Thinley	dge bshes 'phrin las
Jamchen Chöje	byams chen chos rje
Jampa Pel	byams pa dpal
Jampa Thinley	byams pa 'phrin las
Jampel Nyingpo	'jam dpal snying po
Je Pabongka Rinpoche	rje pha bong kha rin po che
Je Tsongkhapa	rje tsong kha pa
Jigten Sumgön	'jig rten gsum dgon
Kadampa	bka' gdams pa
Kagyu(pa)	bka' brgyud (pa)
Kelsang Tenzin	skal bzang bstan 'dzin
Khedrub Je	mkhas grub rje
Khenpo Tsultrim Gyatso	mkhan po tshul khrims rgya mtsho
Khensur Lobsang Tharchin	mkhan zur blo bzang mthar pyin
Kirti Tsenshab Rinpoche	ki rti'i mtshan zhabs rin po che
kun-da da-bu jang-sem	kun da lta bu byang sems
Kyabje Ling Dorjechang	skyabs rje gling rin po che
Kyabje Trijang Dorjechang	skyabs rje khri byang rdo rje 'chang
lam-kyi mang-do	lam gyi rmang rdo
lam-rim	lam rim
Lama Tenzin Osel Rinpoche	bla ma bstan 'dzin 'od gsal rin po che
Lama Thubten Yeshe	bla ma thub bstan ye shes
Lama Thubten Zopa Rinpoche	bla ma thub bstan bzod pa rin po che
Lhasa	lha sa
Losang Chökyi Gyeltsen	blo bzang chos kyi rgyal mtshan
Losang Döndrup	blo bzang don grub
Losang Dragpa	blo bzang grags pa
lung	lung
Lungtok Rinpoche	lung rtogs rin po che
Marpa	mar pa
Mey lineage	mes brgyud
Milarepa	mi la ras pa
Miwang Dragpa Gyaltsen	mi dbang grags pa rgyal mtshan
Mönlam Chenmo	smon lam chen mo
Na-ro chö druk	na ro chos drug
Nada	nāda
Ngawang Jampa	ngag dbang byams pa

Ngawang Jigdol	ngag dbang 'jigs grol
Ngawang Tenpa	ngag dbang bstan pa
Ngok lineage	rngog brgyud
Ngokton	rngog ston
ngöndro	sngon 'gro
Nyingma(pa)	rnying ma (pa)
Pabongka Dechen Nyingpo	pha bong kha bde chen snying po
Padma Dorje	pad ma rdo rje
Pagmo Drupa	phag mo gru pa
Panchen Lama	paṇ chen bla ma
Rechungpa	ras chung (pa)
Sakya Pandita	sa skya paṇḍita
(Kunga Gyaltsen)	(kun dga' rgyal mtshan)
Sakya Trizin	sa skya khri 'dzin
Sakya(pa)	sa skya (pa)
Samten Chhosphel	bsam gten chos 'phel
Sangye Yeshe	sangs rgyas ye shes
Sera (Je)	se ra (byas)
Sönam Senge	bsod nams seng ge
Sönam Wangpo	bsod nams dbang po
sum	gsum
thangka	thang ka
Thubten Ngödrup	thub bstan dgnos grub
Thubten Samphel	thub bstan bsam 'phel
tigle	thig le
torma	gtor ma
Trijang Rinpoche	khri byang rin po che
tsa-tsa	tsha tsha
Tsawa	tsha ba
Tsongkhapa	tsong kha pa
Tsur lineage	mtshur brgyud
Tsurton	mtshur ston
tummo	gtum mo
Wangchug Menkangpa	dbang phyugs sman khang pa
Wolka	'ol kha
Yang Tsewa	yang brtse ba
Yangtse Rinpoche	yang rtse rin po che
Yeshe Gyeltsen	ye shes rgyal mtshan
Yeshe Tenzin	ye shes bstan 'dzin
yi-che	yid ches
yidam	yi dam
Zong Rinpoche	zong rin po che

Outline of *Having the Three Convictions: A Guide to the Stages of the Profound Path of the Six Yogas of Naropa*

I. PRELIMINARY PRACTICES

A. The Common Practices of the Great Vehicle Path in General
   1. *The need for training in the common path even in this system*
   2. *The stages of training the mind in such paths*

B. The Preliminaries of Highest Yoga Tantra, the Uncommon Path
   1. *General preliminaries*
      a. The need to receive a full empowerment
      b. The need to observe the commitments
   2. *Uncommon preliminaries*
      a. Vajrasattva meditation and recitation to purify negativities and obscurations
      b. Meditation on guru yoga to receive inspiring powers
         1) Meditating on the guru as a merit field
         2) Making offerings and beseeching the guru

II. THE MODE OF ACTUAL PRACTICE BASED ON THE PRELIMINARIES

A. Meditations on the Generation Stage

B. Meditations on the Completion Stage
   1. *The nature of the bases*
      a. The nature of the mind
      b. The nature of the body
   2. *The stages of traversing the path*
      a. The practices of the physical yoga exercises and the hollow body as the first step
         1) The physical yoga exercises
            a) Holding one's breath like a filled vase
            b) Rotating like a wheel

    c) Bending the body like a hook

    d) The mudra of vajra binding, throwing up in the air and dropping down

    e) Straightening the spine like an arrow in the manner of a vomiting dog

    f) Shaking the entire body and stretching the joints to enable the smooth flow of blood in the arteries

  2) Visualization of the hollow body

b. The practical stages of the actual subsequent paths

  1) The various modes of dividing the path

  2) The stages of leading on the path

    a) The actual practices of the path

    (1) The main practices of the path

      (a) Drawing the winds into the central channel and generating the four joys

        i) The internal method of inner fire

        (a) The entry of the winds into the central channel through the practice of inner fire

          (i) The practice of inner fire yoga

            a. Visualization of the energy channels

            b. Visualization of the letters

            c. The practice of the vase breath

          (ii) The process of the entering, abiding, and absorption of the winds within the central channel through the practice of inner fire

        (b) The experience of the four joys following the entering of the winds into the central channel

          (i) The arising of signs (associated with the process of dissolution of the elements) and the igniting of the inner fire

          (ii) The experience of the four joys induced by the melting of the bodhicitta drops

          (iii) Meditation on the simultaneously born transcendental wisdom

        ii) The external method of relying on an action seal

      (b) The practices of the clear light and the illusory body based on the generation of the four joys

   i) General discussion of the practices of the remaining
      paths in reliance on the practice of inner fire meditation

  ii) Individual practices of the specific paths

  (a) The practices of the illusory body

    (i) Meditation on the illusory nature of appearances

    (ii) Meditation on the illusory nature of dreams

      a. Recognizing one's dreams as dreams

      b. Training in dream yoga and its enhancement

      c. Overcoming anxieties in dreams and training
         in awareness of their illusory nature

      d. Meditating on the actual nature of dreams

    (iii) Meditation on the illusory nature of the bardo state

      a. General discussion of the bardo state

      b. The stages of the practices related to the bardo
        state

        (1) Types of persons gaining control over the
           bardo existence

        (2) The manner in which such control is gained

  (b) The practices of the clear light

    (i) The practice of the clear light during waking

    (ii) The practice of the clear light during sleep

 (2) The branch practices, the transference (of consciousness)
    and resurrection into a dead body

  (a) Transference (of consciousness) to a higher state

  (b) Resurrection into a dead body

 b) Engaging in the conducts to accelerate the process of the
   path

3. *The mode in which the resultant state is actualized*

This outline was prepared by Geshe Thupten Jinpa for the commentary on *Having the Three Convictions* given by His Holiness the Fourteenth Dalai Lama in Dharamsala, India, from March 22 to 26, 1990.

Notes

FOREWORD

1. Buxa Duar in West Bengal, India, is where most of the Tibetan monks who escaped to India in 1959 were accommodated. It had been a prison camp during the time of British rule in India.

2. Verses 18 and 19 in chapter 3.

CHAPTER 1 TANTRA AND INNER FIRE

1. An alternative listing of the six factors is bone, marrow, and semen received from the father and flesh, blood, and skin received from the mother.

CHAPTER 2 THE SIX YOGAS AND THE MAHASIDDHA NAROPA

1. Lama Yeshe received commentaries on the Six Yogas from both his root guru Kyabje Trijang Rinpoche and His Holiness the Fourteenth Dalai Lama.

2. Marpa gave only the oral instruction transmission of the Six Yogas to Milarepa; however, two other disciples, Ngokton and Tsurton, received the complete teaching, with explanations from the root tantras and commentaries.

CHAPTER 3 THE MAHASIDDHA JE TSONGKHAPA

1. For example, Lama Tsongkhapa completed a four-year Guhyasamaja retreat accompanied by eight disciples in the Wolka Mountains in Tibet. During the retreat he lived on only a handful of juniper berries each day. For further biographical details, see Robert Thurman's *Life and Teachings of Tsong Khapa* (Dharamsala: Library of Tibetan Works and Archives, 1982).

2. *Having the Three Convictions* was composed at the request of two brothers, one of whom, Miwang Dragpa Gyaltsen, was the principal sponsor of the Mönlam Chenmo.

3. The Guhyasamaja mandala contains thirty-three deities.

CHAPTER 4 THE POINT IS TO PRACTICE

1. The three negativities of body are killing, stealing, and sexual misconduct. The four negativities of speech are lying, harsh speech, slander, and gossip. The three negativities of mind are covetousness, ill-will, and wrong views. All together these constitute the ten nonvirtuous actions.

CHAPTER 5 PREPARING THE MIND

1. See Appendix 3 (p. 193) for an outline of *Having the Three Convictions*.

2. Lama Tsongkhapa wrote three commentaries on the lam-rim: the extensive, intermediate, and brief. The extensive is *The Great Exposition of the Stages of the Path to Enlightenment*; the intermediate is *The Middling Exposition of the Stages of the Path to Enlightenment*; and the brief is *Songs of Experience of the Stages of the Path to Enlightenment*.

3. The other six tantric preliminaries are refuge, prostrations, water-bowl offerings, *tsa-tsas*, Dorje Khadro fire pujas, and Samayavajra.

4. The seven-limb practice consists of prostration, offering, confession, rejoicing, requesting teachings, imploring the guru to live long, and dedication.

CHAPTER 7 PURIFYING NEGATIVITIES

1. For further details, see Lama Yeshe's *The Tantric Path of Purification* (Boston: Wisdom Publications, 1995), a collection of commentaries on the yoga method of Heruka Vajrasattva.

CHAPTER 8 THE INSPIRATION OF THE GURU

1. In Tushita, Lama Tsongkhapa manifests as the god Jampel Nyingpo (Wisdom Essence).

2. The mandala offering is an offering of the entire universe to the guru-deity. External offerings involve the offering of material objects, actual or visualized, to the guru-deity; internal offerings refer to the offering of blessed substances visualized as transcendental wisdom nectar; secret offerings refer to the offering to the guru-deity of consorts; and suchness offerings refer to the offering of the realization of emptiness.

3. The final two paths leading to Buddhahood are the paths of meditation and no more learning. See glossary.

CHAPTER 9 TRANSFORMING DEATH, INTERMEDIATE STATE, AND REBIRTH

1. There are four main lineages coming from Marpa: the Mey lineage, the Tsur lineage, the Ngok lineage, and the lineage of Milarepa.

CHAPTER 10 ARISING AS A DIVINE BEING

1. Lama Tsongkhapa mentions that in the practice of the Six Yogas the evolutionary stage is usually based on the mandala of Hevajra or Heruka Chakrasamvara.

CHAPTER 11 THE CHARACTERISTICS OF BODY AND MIND

1. There are five basic winds: (1) the life-bearing wind, which causes inhalation, exhalation, and so forth; (2) the upward-moving wind, which is involved in speech, swallowing, and so forth; (3) the pervasive wind, which enables the limbs to move and so forth; (4) the fire-dwelling wind, which is responsible for digestion and so forth; and (5) the downward-voiding wind, which is responsible for defecation, urination, the emission of semen, and so forth. For further details see *Highest Yoga Tantra* (Ithaca, N.Y.: Snow Lion Publications, 1986) by Daniel Cozort and *Death, Intermediate State, and Rebirth in Tibetan Buddhism* (Ithaca, N.Y.: Snow Lion Publications, 1980) by Lati Rinpochay and Jeffrey Hopkins.

2. For further details see Glenn Mullin's *The Practice of Kalachakra* (Ithaca, N.Y.: Snow Lion Publications, 1991) or His Holiness the Dalai Lama's *The Kalachakra Tantra: Rite of Initiation* (Boston: Wisdom Publications, 1989).

3. In some commentaries, the gross mind is defined as the five sense consciousnesses and the eighty conceptual minds and the subtle mind as the consciousnesses that accompany the white, red, and black visions.

4. The minds that accompany the white, red, and black visions are included in subtle mind because they are conceptual consciousnesses.

CHAPTER 13 HATHA YOGA

1. The other five exercises are (2) rotating like a wheel; (3) bending the body like a hook; (4) the mudra of "vajra binding," throwing up in the air and dropping down; (5) straightening the spine like an arrow in the manner of a vomiting dog; and (6) shaking the entire body and stretching the body and joints to enable a smooth flow of blood in the arteries.

CHAPTER 14 CHANNELS AND CHAKRAS

1. The sixfold knot is formed by the right and left channels crossing the central channel three times, the twofold knot by their crossing the central channel once.

2. According to Kirti Tsenshab Rinpoche, the central channel in the female ends at "the end of the womb where the red drops flow out," that is, the cervix.

3. These are the five Buddha lineages of Akshobhya (blue), Vairochana (white), Ratnasambhava (yellow), Amitabha (red), and Amoghasiddhi (green).

CHAPTER 16 VASE BREATHING MEDITATION

1. In *Having the Three Convictions*, Lama Tsongkhapa actually describes breathing in and out through the right nostril, then the left nostril, then both together. This three-part cycle is then repeated three times to make the nine rounds.

2. In Glenn Mullin's translation of *Having the Three Convictions*, Lama Tsongkhapa says "the vital energies from above and below are to be brought together in a kiss."

CHAPTER 18 GOOD THINGS AND BAD THINGS CAN HAPPEN

1. The life-bearing wind is white; the upward-moving wind is red; the pervasive wind is pale blue; the fire-dwelling wind is green-yellow; and the downward-voiding wind is yellow.

CHAPTER 20 BECOMING VAJRADHARA

1. Lama Tsongkhapa describes as qualified a person of highest capacity who has received pure empowerments; is learned in the guidelines of tantric practice; is skilled in the sadhana of the mandala cycle and in practicing four daily sessions of yoga; is also skilled in the sixty-four arts of love; is experienced in meditation upon emptiness; is experienced in the techniques for inducing the four joys and simultaneously born great wisdom; and can control the melted drops so that there is no emission.

2. Consorts can be classified in various ways; for example, there is a fourfold classification in dependence upon their caste. There is a threefold division in dependence upon the level of their realizations. A mantra-born consort is skilled in evolutionary stage yoga and has achieved realization of the initial stages of completion stage. A place-born consort resides in one of the holy tantric places, such as in one of the twenty-four holy places of Heruka. A simultaneously born consort abides in union with the clear light realization.

Glossary

(Skt = Sanskrit; Tib = Tibetan)

absolute guru. The blissful, omniscient mind of the Buddhas; the dharmakaya.

absolute reality. Nonduality; emptiness; absolute existence; absolute nature; ultimate reality; fundamental nature. The way that the self and all phenomena actually exist—that is, as empty of self-existence.

absolute view. The view of absolute reality.

absorptions. See *death process.*

Action Tantra. In Sanskrit, *Kriya Tantra.* The first of the four classes of tantra, in which the bliss generated by looking at a deity is utilized in the path to enlightenment.

airs. Winds; energy-winds; vital energies. Subtle energies that flow in the channels of the body, which enable the body to function and which are associated with the different levels of mind.

Asanga. The fifth-century Indian pandit who received directly from Maitreya Buddha the extensive, or method, lineage of Shakyamuni Buddha's teachings. His writings are the basis for the Chittamatra school of Buddhist tenets.

Atisha (982–1054). The renowned Indian Buddhist master who came to Tibet to help revive Buddhism, spending the last seventeen years of his life there. Lama Atisha wrote the first lam-rim text, *Lamp on the Path to Enlightenment,* and founded the tradition of the Kadampas, practitioners renowned for their renunciation and bodhicitta.

bhumi (Skt). Literally, stage, or ground. Bodhisattvas must traverse ten bhumis on their journey to enlightenment, the first being reached with their initial non-conceptual realization of nonduality.

Bodhgaya. The small town in the state of Bihar in north India where Shakyamuni Buddha became enlightened.

bodhicitta (Skt). The effortless and continuously present altruistic wish in the minds of bodhisattvas to achieve enlightenment for the sake of all sentient beings. In tantra, bodhicitta also refers to kundalini.

bodhisattva (Skt). One who possesses bodhicitta. A person becomes a bodhisattva when they first achieve effortless bodhicitta.

bodhisattva ordination. The formal taking of bodhisattva vows, a set of Mahayana commitments to dedicate one's life to achieving enlightenment for the benefit of all sentient beings.

Buddha (Skt). An enlightened being.

Buddhadharma. See *Dharma.*

Butön (1312–64). A Sakya scholar-historian and a great yogi; one of the lineage lamas of the Six Yogas of Naropa.

central channel. The most important of the thousands of channels of the subtle body. During inner fire meditation it is visualized as blue, as running just in front of the spine, and as starting at the brow chakra and ending four finger-widths below the navel.

chakras (Skt). Literally, wheels. Formed by the branching of channels at various points along the central channel, the six main chakras are at the brow, crown, throat, heart, navel, and sex organ. The navel chakra is the primary focus during inner fire meditation.

Chandrakirti. The sixth-century Indian pandit, a disciple of Nagarjuna, who eluci-dated Nagarjuna's exposition of Madhyamaka, presenting it specifically as Prasangika-Madhyamaka. Chandrakirti's texts are the basis of the study of Madhyamaka in all Tibetan traditions.

channels. The 72,000 energy channels of the body, which, with the airs and the kundalini, constitute the subtle body, and which are worked with in such prac-tices as inner fire.

Chittamani Tara (Skt). The Highest Yoga Tantra aspect of the female deity Tara.

Chittamatra (Skt). Mind-Only. One of the two main Mahayana schools of Buddhist tenets, for whom subtle selflessness is the nondifference in entity between mind and external phenomena, subject and object.

clear appearance. Clarity. The vivid visualization by the yogi and yogini of themselves as a deity and their surroundings as the deity's mandala. This practice, combined with that of divine pride, is cultivated during the evolutionary stage.

clear light. Very subtle mind; the fourth empty; also refers to the object, emptiness, of the clear light mind; one of the Six Yogas of Naropa. This subtlest state of mind occurs naturally at death, for example, and through successful practice of inner fire, and is used by yogis and yoginis to realize nonduality. When achieved through meditation, this *initial* clear light is then perfected, becom-ing the *actual* clear light, which is unified with the pure illusory body to bring the accomplishment of enlightenment. See also *four empties.*

completion stage. The more advanced of the two stages of Highest Yoga Tantra.

This stage is entered when the yogi or yogini begins to accomplish the entering, stabilizing, and absorbing of the airs in the central channel through practicing methods such as inner fire.

consort. A real or visualized partner used by a yogi or yogini to enhance the experience of simultaneously born bliss.

conventional reality. Conventional existence; relative reality; dependent-arising; interdependent. The way that the self and all phenomena exist conventionally; that is, relatively, interdependently, as dependent arisings.

daka (Skt). The male equivalent of a dakini.

dakini (Skt). Literally, sky-goer. A female being with tantric realizations who helps arouse bliss in a yogi.

death process. The gradual absorption, or dissolution, of the physical and mental faculties of a person that occurs naturally at death. This absorption also occurs during the meditation of a yogi or yogini who causes the airs to enter, stabilize, and absorb in the central channel. Each of the eight stages of the death process is accompanied by an inner sign, or vision. The first four visions, which accompany the absorption of the four elements and the five senses, are the mirage, smoke, sparks or fireflies, and flickering flame. The second four visions are experienced as white light, red light, blackness or darkness, and clear light.

deity. In Tibetan, *yidam.* A divine being, a Buddha, such as Heruka or Vajrayogini.

dependent-arising. Relative; interdependent. The way that the self and all phenomena exist conventionally: they come into being in dependence upon 1) causes and conditions, 2) their parts, and, most subtly, 3) the mind imputing or labeling them.

Dharma (Skt). Buddhadharma. In general, spiritual practice; specifically, the Buddhist teachings, which protect from suffering and lead to liberation and full enlightenment.

dharmakaya (Skt). See *three kayas.*

divine pride. The yogi's or yogini's strong conviction that they actually are the deity they are visualizing themselves as in their meditation. This practice, combined with that of clear appearance, is cultivated during the evolutionary stage.

dream yoga. Part of illusory body yoga, in which the yogi or yogini transforms their dream body into the body of the deity and performs spiritual practice.

Drilbupa. Also known as Ghantapa; one of the Eighty-four Mahasiddhas and founder of one of the three main Heruka Chakrasamvara lineages.

Dromtönpa (1005–64). Lama Atisha's heart disciple and chief translator in Tibet; propagator of the Kadampa tradition.

drops. See *kundalini.*

dualistic. See *self-existence.*

eighty superstitions. Eighty conceptual minds; eighty indicative conceptions. Various conceptual states of mind that dissolve at the time of death before the fifth stage, the mind of white appearance. For a list of the eighty superstitions, see pp. 39–41 in *Death, Intermediate State, and Rebirth in Tibetan Buddhism* (Ithaca, N.Y.: Snow Lion Publications, 1980) by Lati Rinbochay and Jeffrey Hopkins.

Eighty-four Mahasiddhas. Great yogis of ancient India, such as Nagarjuna, Tilopa, Naropa, Drilbupa, and Luhipa, who through their practice of tantra attained enlightenment in a single lifetime and brought about the flowering of the Tantrayana.

empowerment. See *initiation.*

emptiness. See *nonduality.*

enlightenment. Buddhahood; omniscience; totality; full enlightenment; awakening; Vajradharahood; Herukahood; unification. The ultimate goal of Mahayana Buddhist practice and the potential of all sentient beings, enlightenment is characterized by infinite wisdom, infinite compassion, and infinite power. In tantra, it is the final union of the actual clear light and pure illusory body.

evolutionary stage. Generation stage. The first of the two stages of Highest Yoga Tantra, during which the yogi or yogini practices transforming the ordinary experiences of death, intermediate state, and rebirth into the pure experiences of the dharmakaya, sambhogakaya, and nirmanakaya; and then, by visualizing themselves as that nirmanakaya deity, they cultivate the clear appearance and divine pride of actually being that divine being.

external offering. The offerings of material objects, actual or visualized, to the guru-deity.

father tantra. The tantras, such as Guhyasamaja, that emphasize the practice of the illusory body.

five Buddha families. The five Buddha lineages: Akshobhya, Vairochana, Ratnasambhava, Amitabha, and Amoghasiddhi. They represent 1) the purification of the five contaminated aggregates, 2) the purification of the delusions of anger, ignorance, pride, desire, and jealousy, and 3) the attainment of the five transcendental wisdoms.

four elements. Earth, water, fire, and air; together with the channels and the kundalini, these constitute the six distinctive characteristics of the human body. They are the constituents of all physical phenomena.

four empties. Four subtle types of consciousness—the minds of white appearance, red increase, black near-attainment, and clear light—which occur naturally at death, for example, or as a result of successful inner fire meditation when the airs have absorbed in the central channel. These subtle minds are used by the yogi or yogini to realize nonduality.

four initiations. The vase, secret, wisdom, and word initiations, which are prerequisites for practice of the evolutionary and completion stages of Highest Yoga Tantra. The latter three initiations are unique to Highest Yoga Tantra.

four joys. Four blisses. Bliss consciousnesses generated by the yogi or yogini after the airs have absorbed in the central channel and heat has been generated through successful inner fire meditation, causing the kundalini at the crown to melt. It flows down the central channel to the throat, heart, navel, and secret chakras, culminating in the fourth joy, known as simultaneously born bliss. The four joys of the reverse order are experienced when the kundalini is brought back up through the chakras to the crown.

Four Noble Truths. The subject of Shakyamuni Buddha's first discourse: true suffering, true cause of suffering, true cessation of suffering, and true path to the cessation of suffering.

Gampopa (1079–1153). One of the chief disciples of Milarepa, a lineage lama of the Six Yogas of Naropa, and author of *The Jewel Ornament of Liberation,* a renowned lam-rim text.

Ganden Monastery. The first of the three great Gelugpa monastic universities near Lhasa, founded in 1409 by Lama Je Tsongkhapa. It was destroyed in the 1960s and has now been reestablished in exile in south India.

Gelug (Tib). One of the four traditions of Tibetan Buddhism, it was founded by Lama Je Tsongkhapa in the early fifteenth century and has been propagated by such illustrious masters as the successive Dalai Lamas and Panchen Lamas.

Gelugpa (Tib). A follower of the Gelug tradition.

Gen (Tib). Literally, elder. A title of respect.

Geshe (Tib). Literally, spiritual friend. The title conferred on those who have completed extensive studies and examinations at Gelug monastic universities.

Geshe Lama Könchog. An ascetic meditator and friend of Lama Yeshe; currently lives at Kopan Monastery in Nepal.

Geshe Sopa Rinpoche. An eminent Buddhist scholar and guru of both Lama Yeshe and Lama Zopa Rinpoche; recently retired after serving thirty years as professor of South Asian Studies at the University of Wisconsin (U.S.A.).

Ghantapa. See *Drilbupa.*

gross body. The blood, bones, sense organs, and so forth that make up the ordinary physical body.

gross mind. The five sense consciousnesses.

Guhyasamaja (Skt). A male deity of Highest Yoga Tantra, belonging to father tantra. The Guhyasamaja tantra is known as the King of Tantras because of its extensive instructions, especially on the illusory body. The main meditational deity of Lama Je Tsongkhapa.

guru (Skt). In Tibetan, *lama.* Literally, heavy, as in heavy with Dharma knowledge. One's spiritual guide, teacher, or master.

Guru Heruka. The tantric guru seen as inseparably one with Heruka.

Guru Vajradhara. The tantric guru seen as inseparably one with Vajradhara.

guru yoga (Skt). The tantric practice in which the yogi or yogini meditates on the guru and the deity as being inseparably one, and then merges this guru-deity with their own mind; the various sadhanas that incorporate these meditations

hatha yoga (Skt). The physical exercises known as the Six Magical Wheels taught in the Six Yogas of Naropa. These help the practitioner to succeed in inner fire meditation by removing the blockages that impede the flow of the energies in the channels. (1) vase breathing; (2) rotating like a wheel; (3) bending the body like a hook; (4) the mudra of "vajra binding," throwing up in the air and dropping down; (5) straightening the spine like an arrow in the manner of a vomiting dog; and (6) shaking the entire body and stretching the body and joints to enable a smooth flow of blood in the arteries.

Heruka (Skt). Heruka Chakrasamvara. A male meditational deity of Highest Yoga Tantra, belonging to mother tantra, whose tantra especially emphasizes the clear light.

Heruka Body-Mandala. A practice in which Guru Heruka's body is visualized as the parts of the mandala.

Hevajra (Skt). A male meditational deity of Highest Yoga Tantra, belonging to mother tantra.

Highest Yoga Tantra. In Sanskrit, *Maha-anuttara Yoga Tantra.* The fourth and supreme class of tantra, consisting of evolutionary and completion stages, which must be accomplished in order to achieve enlightenment.

Hinayana (Skt). Literally, the Lesser Vehicle. The path of the arhats, the goal of which is nirvana, or personal liberation from samsara.

illusory body. A body made of subtle air energies in the form of a deity but white in color; one of the Six Yogas of Naropa. The yogi or yogini arises in an impure illusory body immediately after their initial experience of clear light and in a pure illusory body after the achievement of the actual clear light.

indestructible drop. The red and white drop, the size of a mustard seed, located in the central channel in the heart chakra. It contains the very subtle mind and wind.

inherent existence. See *self-existence.*

initiation. Empowerment. The transmission of the practice of a particular deity from a tantric master to a disciple, which permits the disciple to engage in that practice.

inner fire. In Tibetan, *tummo*; literally, brave female. This is the first of the Six Yogas of Naropa. A completion stage tantric meditation technique for bringing all the airs into the central channel, thus awakening the clear light mind. If successfully accomplished, the process can lead to enlightenment in one lifetime.

inner offering. Blessed offering substances visualized as transcendental wisdom nectar and offered to the guru-deity.

intermediate state. In Tibetan, *bardo.* The state between death and rebirth, lasting anywhere from a moment to forty-nine days.

internal offering. See *inner offering.*

Jampa Wangdu (d. 1984). An ascetic meditator who was a close friend of Lama Yeshe and a guru of Lama Zopa Rinpoche; Lungtok Rinpoche, a Chinese boy from Hong Kong, has been recognized by His Holiness the Dalai Lama as his reincarnation.

Kagyu (Tib). One of the four traditions of Tibetan Buddhism, having its source in such illustrious lineage lamas as Marpa, Milarepa, and Gampopa.

Kagyupa (Tib). A follower of the Kagyu tradition.

Kalachakra (Skt). A male deity of Highest Yoga Tantra. The Kalachakra Tantra contains instructions in medicine, astronomy, and so forth.

karma (Skt). Literally, action. The law of cause and effect: the process whereby positive actions of body, speech, and mind lead to happiness and negative ones to suffering.

Khedrub Je (1385–1438). One of Lama Je Tsongkhapa's heart disciples and the leading propagator of his tantric teachings, he follows Lama Tsongkhapa in the lineage of the Six Yogas of Naropa. He was the third Ganden Tripa, or Holder of the Ganden Throne.

kundalini (Skt). In Tibetan *tigle*; drops; blissful energy; also referred to as bodhicitta. Red and white subtle liquid energy that exists throughout the channels of the body, the red predominating at the navel chakra and the white at the crown chakra.

Kyabje (Tib). Literally, lord of refuge. A title of respect.

lama (Tib). See *guru*.

Lama Chöpa (Tib). Or, in Sanskrit, *Guru Puja*; an extensive guru yoga practice involving prayers, requests, and offerings to the lama.

Lama Je Tsongkhapa (1357–1419). The mahasiddha, scholar, and teacher who founded the Gelug tradition of Tibetan Buddhism; author of many texts, including the commentary on the Six Yogas of Naropa called *Having the Three Convictions.*

Lama Tsongkhapa Guru Yoga. A guru yoga practice related to Lama Je Tsongkhapa that is performed daily in Gelugpa monasteries.

lam-rim (Tib). Literally, graduated path. Originally outlined in Tibet by the eleventh-century master Lama Atisha in *Lamp on the Path to Enlightenment,* the lam-rim is a step-by-step arrangement of Buddha's teachings, presented as meditations to be actualized. It incorporates Hinayana, Paramitayana, and Tantrayana.

left channel. The channel to the left of the central channel. During inner fire meditation, it is visualized as white and as starting at the left nostril and curving into the central channel four finger-widths below the navel.

liberation. Nirvana, the state beyond sorrow; liberation from suffering through abandonment of all delusions; the goal of the Hinayana practitioner.

lineage lamas. The spiritual teachers who constitute the line of direct guru-disciple transmission of teachings, from Buddha to the teachers of the present day.

Ling Dorjechang (1903–83). Ling Rinpoche. The late Senior Tutor to His Holiness the Fourteenth Dalai Lama. He was the Ninety-seventh Holder of the Ganden Throne.

Lord Buddha. See *Shakyamuni Buddha.*

lower doors. The anal, urethral, and vaginal openings.

lower realms. See *samsara.*

Luhipa. One of the Eighty-four Mahasiddhas and founder of one of the three main lineages of Heruka Chakrasamvara practice.

lung (Tib). Literally, wind. The state in which the airs of the body are unbalanced or blocked, thus causing various illnesses.

mahamudra (Skt). Literally, great seal. In sutra, it refers to the emptiness of the mind; in tantra, it refers to the union of simultaneously born wisdom and emptiness. Mahamudra also refers to the types of meditation for developing these realizations.

mahasiddha (Skt). An accomplished tantric yogi; a saint.

Mahayana (Skt). Literally, the Great Vehicle. The path of the bodhisattvas, the ultimate goal of which is Buddhahood; includes both Paramitayana and Tantrayana.

Maitripa. An eleventh-century Indian mahasiddha, famous for his mastery of mahamudra, who was one of Marpa's main gurus.

mandala (Skt). The purified environment of a tantric deity; the diagram or painting representing this.

mandala offerings. The visualized offering to the guru-deity of the entire universe; one of the tantric preliminaries.

Manjushri (Skt). A male deity embodying the wisdom of nonduality. Lama Je Tsongkhapa received teachings directly from Manjushri.

Mantrayana. See *Tantrayana.*

mantra (Skt). Literally, protection of the mind. The mind is protected from ordinary appearances and conceptions, from seeing oneself and other phenomena as mundane; Sanskrit syllables recited in conjunction with the practice of a particular deity that embody the qualities of that deity.

Marpa (1012–99). The translator and yogi who was a disciple of Naropa and the main guru of Milarepa. The founder of the Kagyu tradition, Marpa was the holder of many tantric lineages and brought the lineage of the Six Yogas of Naropa to Tibet.

Milarepa (1040–1123). The ascetic Tibetan yogi and poet, foremost disciple of Marpa, who was famous for his intensive practice, his devotion to his guru, his many songs of spiritual realization, and his attainment of enlightenment in one lifetime. An important lineage lama in the transmission of the Six Yogas of Naropa.

mother tantra. The tantras that emphasize the practice of clear light, such as Heruka and Hevajra.

mudra (Skt). Literally, gesture. Symbolic hand gestures used during various tantric rituals. Mudra can also refer to the consort.

nada (Skt). A fine line with three curves, sometimes called a squiggle, visualized above the syllable at each chakra during inner fire meditation.

Nagarjuna. The Indian scholar and tantric adept, born approximately four hundred years after Buddha's parinirvana, who, in propounding the Madhyamaka, elucidated the meaning of Buddha's teachings on emptiness.

Nalanda. A Mahayana Buddhist monastic university founded in the fifth century in north India, not far from Bodhgaya, which served as a major source of the Buddhist teachings that spread to Tibet. Naropa was the abbot of Nalanda for eight years.

Naropa (1016–1100). The Indian mahasiddha who transmitted many tantric lineages, including those of Heruka and Vajrayogini; disciple of Tilopa and guru of Marpa and Maitripa.

natural negativities. Negative actions other than those created by breaking any of the three sets of vows: individual liberation, bodhisattva, or tantric.

nine mixings. Performed during waking, sleeping, and dying, these are the main methods for taking ordinary death, the intermediate state, and rebirth as the paths to the three kayas. They are essential practices of completion stage meditation.

nirmanakaya (Skt). See *three kayas.*

nirvana (Skt). See *liberation.*

nonduality. Emptiness; non-self-existence; fundamental nature; totality. Nonduality is the absolute nature of the self and all phenomena; ultimately, everything is empty of existing dualistically, inherently, truly, or from its own side.

nonduality wisdom. The realization of nonduality.

non-self-existence. See *nonduality.*

Nyingma (Tib). The oldest of the four traditions of Tibetan Buddhism, which traces its teachings back to Guru Padmasambhava, the powerful eighth-century Indian yogi.

Nyingmapa (Tib). A follower of the Nyingma tradition.

Pabongka Rinpoche (1871–1941). Je Pabongka; Pabongka Dechen Nyingpo. An influential and powerful Gelugpa lama and an emanation of Heruka Chakrasamvara; the main guru of the Senior and Junior Tutors of His Holiness the Fourteenth Dalai Lama.

Pagmo Drupa (1110–70). The chief disciple of Gampopa and one of the lineage lamas of the Six Yogas of Naropa.

pandit (Skt). A great scholar and philosopher.

Paramitayana (Skt). Literally, Perfection Vehicle. The bodhisattva vehicle; a section of the Mahayana sutra teachings; one of the two forms of Mahayana, the other being Tantrayana.

path of accumulation. The first of the five paths leading to Buddhahood; the other four are the paths of preparation, seeing, meditation, and no more learning.

Mahayana sutra and tantra practitioners enter the path of accumulation when they first realize bodhicitta.

path of meditation. The fourth of the five paths leading to Buddhahood. Mahayana sutra practitioners enter the path of meditation when they begin deepening and enhancing their direct perception of emptiness and tantric practitioners when they attain a learner's union of the pure illusory body and the actual clear light.

path of no more learning. The fifth of the five paths, the actual attainment of Buddhahood; in tantra known as the non-learner's union of the pure illusory body and actual clear light.

path of preparation. The second of the five paths leading to Buddhahood. Mahayana sutra practitioners enter this path when they first experience the union of calm abiding and special insight with nonduality as the object and tantric practitioners when they begin to experience the entry, stabilization, and absorption of the airs in the central channel.

path of seeing. The third of the five paths to Buddhahood, it is entered by Mahayana sutra practitioners when they first realize nonduality directly and by tantric practitioners when they first experience the actual clear light.

Performance Tantra. In Sanskrit, *Charya Tantra.* The second of the four classes of tantra, in which the bliss experienced through smiling and laughing with a deity is utilized in the path to enlightenment.

Prasangika-Madhyamaka (Skt). Literally, Consequentialist Middle Way. This is the higher of the two Madhyamaka schools of Buddhist tenets. It asserts that nothing whatsoever exists from the side of the self or any other phenomenon, either absolutely or conventionally. This is the view of subtle selflessness adopted by most Tibetan Buddhist traditions.

prostrations. Paying respect to the guru-deity with body, speech, and mind; one of the tantric preliminaries.

protectors. Worldly or enlightened beings who protect Buddhism and its practitioners.

pure lands. Blissful states of existence beyond samsara, each of which is associated with its own Buddha. A practitioner is reborn in a pure land through the force of meditation and prayer and can continue to gain realizations of the path to enlightenment.

purification. The removal, or cleansing, from the mind of negative karma and its imprints.

refuge. The heartfelt reliance upon Buddha, Dharma, and Sangha for guidance on the path to enlightenment.

relative. Dependent-arising; interdependent. The way that the self and all phenomena exist conventionally: they come into being, arise, in dependence upon (1) causes and conditions, (2) their parts, and, most subtly, (3) upon the mind imputing or labeling them.

relic pills. Small pearl-like pills that manifest spontaneously from holy objects such as statues, stupas, relics, or the cremated bodies of great yogis or yoginis.

renunciation. The continuously present wish to be free from the sufferings of samsara, based on the realization that ordinary happiness is without essence.

right channel. The channel to the right of the central channel. During inner fire meditation, it is visualized as red and as starting at the right nostril and curving into the central channel four finger-widths below the navel.

right view. The view of absolute reality.

Rinpoche (Tib). Literally, precious one. An honorific term given to recognized reincarnate lamas; a respectful title used for one's own guru or other lamas.

sadhana (Skt). Literally, method of accomplishment. The step-by-step set of meditations and prayers related to a particular deity practice.

sadhu (Skt). A wandering Hindu yogi.

Sakya (Tib). One of the four traditions of Tibetan Buddhism, it was founded in the eleventh century by Drokmi Shakya Yeshe (933–1047).

Sakyapa. A follower of the Sakya tradition.

Sakya Pandita (1182–1251). The title of Kunga Gyaltsen, a master of the Sakya tradition, who spread Tibetan Buddhism in Mongolia.

samadhi (Skt). Literally, mental stabilization. The state of deep meditative absorption of the yogi or yogini who has achieved single-pointed concentration, which is the ability to focus effortlessly and for as long as they wish on an object of meditation.

samaya (Skt). A yogi or yogini's pledge to keep their vows and commitments.

sambhogakaya (Skt). See *three kayas.*

samsara (Skt). Cyclic existence. There are six samsaric realms: the lower realms of the hell beings, hungry ghosts, and animals and the upper realms of the humans, demigods, and gods. Samsara also refers to the continuous process of death and rebirth within these six realms under the control of karma and delusions. It is also the contaminated aggregates, the body and mind of a sentient being.

Sautrantika (Skt). The Scripturalists, one of the two Hinayana schools of Buddhist tenets. They assert that subtle selflessness is the emptiness of a self-sufficient and substantial self.

secret offering. The offering of consorts to the guru-deity.

seed-syllable. Syllable; letter. A Sanskrit letter, such as *haṃ* or *oṃ*, which is visualized at the chakras during meditation practices such as inner fire.

self-existence. Dualistic existence; inherent existence; true existence. The type of existence that the self and all phenomena appear to have and that ignorance believes in. In fact, everything that exists is empty of even an atom of self-existence.

sentient being. Any being in the six realms; according to the Mahayana, one who has not yet reached enlightenment.

Sera Monastery. One of the three great Gelugpa monastic universities near Lhasa, founded in the early fifteenth century by Jamchen Chöje, a disciple of Lama Je Tsongkhapa; now also established in exile in south India.

Shakyamuni Buddha (563–483 B.C.E.). The fourth of the one thousand founding Buddhas of this present world age, Lord Buddha was born a prince of the Shakya clan in North India, renounced his kingdom, achieved enlightenment at the age of twenty-nine, and then taught the paths to liberation and enlightenment until he passed away at the age of eighty.

short a. (Tib. *a tung*) The syllable visualized at the navel chakra that is the main object of concentration during inner fire meditation. (This term is used to differentiate the Sanskrit vowel "a" (pronounced as in but) from the long vowel ā (pronounced as in father).)

simultaneously born bliss. Simultaneously born great bliss; the fourth joy. A sublime state of bliss experienced by the yogi or yogini when, through successful inner fire meditation, the airs have entered, stabilized, and absorbed in the central channel and the kundalini at the crown has melted and flowed down the central channel to the tip secret chakra. This bliss is also experienced when the kundalini is brought back up the central channel to the crown.

simultaneously born great blissful wisdom. Simultaneously born blissful wisdom; simultaneously born wisdom; the wisdom realizing nonduality unified with simultaneously born bliss.

single-pointed concentration. See *samadhi.*

six perfections of a bodhisattva. The practices to be perfected during the ten bodhisattva bhumis: generosity, morality, patience, enthusiastic perseverance, concentration, and wisdom.

Six Magical Wheels. See *hatha yoga.*

six root delusions. Desire, anger, ignorance, pride, doubt, and wrong views.

Six Yogas of Naropa. A set of completion stage tantric practices, listed by Lama Je Tsongkhapa in *Having the Three Convictions* as inner fire meditation, the yoga of the illusory body, the yoga of clear light, transference of consciousness, transference into another body, and the yoga of the intermediate state.

subtle body. Vajra body. The system of channels, airs, and kundalini drops within a human body.

subtle mind. The conceptual states of mind, such as anger, desire, and so forth.

suchness offering. The offering of the realization of emptiness to the guru-deity.

sutra (Skt). The Hinayana and Paramitayana discourses of Buddha; the open discourses; a scriptural text and the teachings and practices it contains.

Sutrayana (Skt). The non-tantric vehicle of Buddhism as outlined in the Hinayana and Mahayana sutras.

Svatantrika-Madhyamaka (Skt). Literally, Autonomous Middle Way. One of the two Madhyamaka schools of Buddhist tenets within the Mahayana, which asserts that although the self and all phenomena lack true existence, conventionally they do exist from their own side.

tantra (Skt). The secret teachings of Lord Buddha (see *Tantrayana*); a scriptural text and the teachings and practices it contains.

Tantrayana (Skt). Vajrayana; Mantrayana; Secret Mantra; the quick path. The secret teachings of Lord Buddha, given by him in the aspect of Vajradhara; the advanced stages of the Mahayana path to enlightenment, successful practice of which can lead to enlightenment in one lifetime.

tantric preliminaries. The practices that prepare the mind for successful tantric meditation by removing hindrances and accumulating merit, thus qualifying the yogi or yogini to practice tantra.

thangkas (Tib). Painted or appliquéd depictions of deities, usually set in a framework of colorful brocade.

Thirty-five Buddhas of Confession. The group of thirty-five buddhas visualized while reciting *The Sutra of the Three Heaps* and performing prostrations.

three appearances. See *three visions.*

three kayas (Skt). The three bodies of a Buddha: *dharmakaya* (truth body) is the blissful, omniscient mind of a Buddha; *sambhogakaya* (enjoyment body) is the subtle light-body of a deity, in which a Buddha appears to bodhisattvas; and *nirmanakaya* (emanation body) is the form in which the Buddha appears to ordinary beings.

three poisonous minds. Desire, anger, and ignorance, the three main delusions from the six root delusions.

three principal paths. The essential points of the lam-rim: renunciation, bodhicitta, and emptiness, or right view.

three visions. Three appearances. The white vision, red vision, and black vision, which are the appearances to the first three of the four empties.

Tilopa (988–1069). Tenth-century Indian mahasiddha and guru of Naropa; source of many lineages of tantric teachings.

torma (Tib). A ritual cake (traditionally made from roasted barley flour, butter, and sugar) that is offered to the Buddhas and other holy beings during religious ceremonies.

totality. See *enlightenment.*

transference into another body. The method used by a yogi or yogini to transfer their mind into the body of someone who has just died and thus revive it; one of the Six Yogas of Naropa.

transference of consciousness. The method used by a yogi or yogini to transfer their mind to a pure land at the time of death; one of the Six Yogas of Naropa.

Trijang Rinpoche (1901–81). The late Junior Tutor of His Holiness the Fourteenth Dalai Lama and root guru of Lama Thubten Yeshe. He was considered an emanation of Heruka Chakrasamvara. The reincarnation of Trijang Rinpoche was born in India in 1983.

tummo (Tib). See *inner fire.*

Tushita Pure Land. The Joyous Land. The pure land of the thousand Buddhas of this eon, where the future Buddha Maitreya presently resides.

twenty branch delusions. A group of mental factors, or states of mind, within the group of fifty-one, which are related to one or more of the six root delusions.

unification. Enlightenment; the final union of the actual clear light and pure illusory body.

Vaibashika. The Great Exposition school, one of the two principal Hinayana schools of Buddhist tenets. See *Sautrantika.*

vajra and bell. Implements used during tantric rituals: the vajra, held in the right hand, symbolizes bliss and the bell, held in the left, nonduality; together they symbolize the union of bliss and nonduality.

Vajrabhairava. See *Yamantaka.*

vajra body. See *subtle body.*

Vajradhara (Skt). The tantric aspect of Shakyamuni Buddha.

Vajrasattva (Skt). A male tantric deity used especially for purification. Meditation on Vajrasattva and recitation of his mantra is one of the tantric preliminaries.

Vajravarahi (Skt). The consort of Heruka Chakrasamvara.

Vajrayana (Skt). See *Tantrayana.*

Vajrayogini (Skt). A female deity of Highest Yoga Tantra, belonging to the Heruka Chakrasamvara cycle of mandalas.

Vasubandhu. An Indian Buddhist scholar of the fifth century; brother of Asanga.

very subtle body. The very subtle wind that is inseparable from the very subtle mind in the indestructible drop in the heart chakra.

very subtle mind. Clear light mind. The subtlest level of mind, it resides in the indestructible drop at the heart chakra and is awakened through such practices as inner fire.

vital energies. See *airs.*

water-bowl offerings. Bowls filled with water, which is visualized as various offerings to the senses, and offered to the guru-deity; one of the tantric preliminaries.

winds. See *airs.*

worldly realizations. Extraordinary powers, such as the ability to fly and to see incredible distances, that can be developed through meditation.

Yamantaka (Skt). Vajrabhairava. The wrathful male deity that is the Highest Yoga Tantra aspect of Manjushri.

yoga (Skt). Literally, to yoke. The spiritual discipline to which one yokes oneself in order to achieve enlightenment.

Yoga Tantra. The third of the four classes of Buddhist tantra, in which the bliss experienced by holding hands and embracing is used in the path to enlightenment.

yogi (Skt). An accomplished male tantric meditator.

yogini (Skt). An accomplished female tantric meditator.

Zong Rinpoche (1905–84). A powerful Gelugpa lama renowned for his wrathful aspect, who had impeccable knowledge of Tibetan Buddhist rituals, art, and science.

Bibliography

"P" refers to *The Tibetan Tripiaka*, Peking Edition, Tibetan Tripiaka Research Institute, Tokyo and Kyoto, 1956.

For canonical works, "Toh" refers to *A Complete Catalogue of the Tibetan Buddhist Canons* (Sendai: Tohoku Imperial University Press, 1934), an index to the Derge edition of the *bKa' 'gyur and bsTan 'gyur*. For the works of Tsongkhapa, "Toh" refers to *A Catalogue of the Tohoku University Collection of Tibetan Works on Buddhism* (Sendai: Seminary of Indology, Tohoku University, 1953).

Atisha
Lamp on the Path to Enlightenment
  bodhipathapradīpa
  byang chub lam gyi sgron ma
    Toh.3947; P.5343, vol.103
    English Translations:
    Richard Sherburne, *A Lamp for the Path and Commentary* (London: Allen and Unwin, 1983).
    Geshe Sonam Rinchen and Ruth Sonam, *Atisha's Lamp for the Path to Enlightenment* (Ithaca: Snow Lion, 1997).

Chandrakirti
Guide to the Middle Way
  madhyamakāvatāra
  dbu ma la 'jug pa
    Toh.3861; P.5262, vol.98
    English Translations:
    C. W. Huntington, Jr. *The Emptiness of Emptiness* (Honolulu: University of Hawaii Press, 1989).
    Jeffrey Hopkins, *Compassion in Tibetan Buddhism* (Ithaca: Snow Lion, 1980). [chapters 1-5]
    Geshe Rabten and Stephen Batchelor, *Echoes of Voidness* (London: Wisdom, 1983). [chapter 6]

Maitreya
Ornament of Clear Realizations
  abhisamayālamkāra
  mngon par rtogs pa'i rgyan
    Toh.3786; P.5184, vol.88
    English Translation:
    Edward Conze, *Abhisamayālamkāra,* Serie Orientale Roma VI (Rome:
    I.S.M.E.O., 1954)

Maitripa [Advayavajra; Maitrīpāda]
Ten Reflections on Simple Suchness
  tattvadaśaka
  de kho na nyid bcu pa
    Toh.2236/54; P.3080, vol.68

Nagarjuna
The Five Stages
  pañcakrama
  rim pa lnga pa
    Toh.1802; P.2667, vol.61

Pabongka Rinpoche, Dechen Nyingpo
Collection of Notes
  gsung thor bu
    in *Collected Works of Pha-boṅ-kha-pa Byams-pa-bstan-'dzin-phrin-las-rgya-
      mtsho* (New Delhi, 1972).

The Yoga of the Three Purifications
  dpal 'khor lo sdom pa'i dag pa gsum gyi rnal 'byor
    in *bla ma'i rnal 'kyor dang, yi dam khag gi bdag bskyed sogs zhal 'don*
      (Dharamsala: Tibetan Cultural Printing Pr., n.d.), pp.322–32.

Shakyamuni Buddha
The Diamond Rosary Tantra
  vajrajñāna-samuccaya-tantra
  ye shes rdo rje kun las btus pa
    Toh.447; P.84, vol.3

The Essential Ornament
  vajra-hṛdayālaṃkāra-tantra
  rdo rje snying po rgyan gyi rgyud
    Toh.451; P.86, vol.3

The Hevajra Tantra in Two Sections
  hevajra-tantra-rāja
  kye'i rdo rje
    Toh.417/8; P.10, vol.1
    English Translations:
    David Snellgrove, *The Hevajra Tantra* (London: Oxford, 1959).
    G. W. Farrow and I. Menon, *The Concealed Essence of the Hevajra Tantra*
    (New Delhi: Motilal Banarsidass, 1992).

Shantideva
A Guide to the Bodhisattva's Way of Life
  bodhisatttvacaryāvatāra
  byang chub sems dpa'i spyod pa la 'jug pa
    Toh.3871; P.5272, vol.99
    English Translations:
    Stephen Batchelor, *A Guide to the Bodhisattva's Way of Life* (Dharamsala:
    Library of Tibetan Works and Archives, 1979).
    Padmakara Translation Group, *The Way of the Bodhisattva* (Boston:
    Shambhala, 1997).
    Vesna A. Wallace and B. Alan Wallace, *A Guide to the Bodhisattva Way of
    Life* (Ithaca: Snow Lion, 1997).

Tsongkhapa
*Having the Three Convictions: A Guide to the Stages of the Profound Path of the Six
    Yogas of Naropa*
  zab lam na ro'i chos drug gi sgo nas 'khrid pa'i rim pa yid ches gsum ldan
    P.6202, vol.160; Toh.5317; Collected Works vol.9 (Ta)
    English Translation:
    Glenn H. Mullin, *Tsongkhapa's Six Yogas of Naropa* (Ithaca: Snow Lion,
    1996).

The Great Exposition of the Stages of the Path to Enlightenment
  *lam rim chen mo; skyes bu gsum gyi rnyams su blang ba'i rim pa thams cad
    tshang bar stong pa'i byang chub lam gyi rim pa*
    P.6001, vol.152; Toh.5392; Collected Works vol.13 (Pa)
    English Translations:
    Alex Wayman, *Calming the Mind and Discerning the Real* (New York:
    Columbia, 1978). [partial translation]
    Elizabeth Napper, *Dependent-Arising and Emptiness* (Boston: Wisdom, 1989).
    [excerpts]

*Lamp Thoroughly Illuminating (Nagarjuna's) The Five Stages: Quintessential
    Instructions of the King of Tantras, the Glorious Guhyasamaja*

rgyud kyi rgyal po dpal gsang ba 'dus pa'i man ngag rim pa lnga rab tu gsal ba'i
sgron me
P.6167, vol.158; Toh.5302; Collected Works vol.7 (Ja)

The Middling Exposition of the Stages of the Path to Enlightenment
lam rim chung ba
P.6002, vol.152–53; Toh.5393; Collected Works vol.14 (Pha)
English Translation:
Elizabeth Napper, *Dependent-Arising and Emptiness* (Boston: Wisdom,
1989). [excerpts]

Songs of Experience, Concise Meaning of the Stages of the Path to Enlightenment
byang chub lam gyi rim pa'i nyams len gyi rnam gzhag mdor bsdus te brjed byang
du bya ba; lam rim bsdus don
P.6061, vol.153; Toh.5275(59); Collected Works vol.2 (Kha)
English Translations:
Sherpa Tulku, Khamlung Tulku, Alexander Berzin and Jonathan Landaw,
Lines of Experience (Dharamsala: Library of Tibetan Works and Archives,
1973).
Geshe Wangyal, *The Door of Liberation* (Boston: Wisdom, 1995) pp.173–81.

Suggested Further Reading

Chang, Garma C. C., trans. *The Hundred Thousand Songs of Milarepa*. Vols. 1 and 2. Boulder: Shambhala, 1979.

Cozort, Daniel. *Highest Yoga Tantra: An Introduction to the Esoteric Buddhism of Tibet*. Ithaca, N.Y.: Snow Lion, 1986.

Guenther, H. V. *The Life and Teachings of Naropa*. London: Oxford University, 1963.

Gyatso, Tenzin, the Fourteenth Dalai Lama. *The Buddhism of Tibet*. Translated and edited by Jeffrey Hopkins. Ithaca, N.Y.: Snow Lion, 1987.

———. *Kalachakra Tantra: Rite of Initiation*. Translated and edited by Jeffrey Hopkins. 2nd ed. Boston: Wisdom, 1989.

———. *Opening the Eye of New Awareness*. Translated by Donald S. Lopez, Jr. Boston: Wisdom, 1985.

———. *The Union of Bliss & Emptiness: A Commentary on the Lama Choepa Guru Yoga Practice*. Translated by Thupten Jinpa. Ithaca, N.Y.: Snow Lion, 1988.

———. *The World of Tibetan Buddhism: An Overview of Its Philosophy and Practice*. Translated, edited, and annotated by Geshe Thupten Jinpa. Boston: Wisdom, 1995.

Gyatso, Tenzin, the Fourteenth Dalai Lama, and Alexander Berzin. *The Gelug/Kagyü Tradition of Mahamudra*. Ithaca, N.Y.: Snow Lion, 1997.

Hopkins, Jeffrey. *Meditation on Emptiness*. London: Wisdom, 1984.

Kongtrul, Jamgon. *Creation and Completion: Essential Points of Tantric Meditation*. Translated, annotated, and introduced by Sarah Harding. Boston: Wisdom, 1996.

Landaw, Jonathan, and Andy Weber. *Images of Enlightenment: Tibetan Art in Practice*. Ithaca, N.Y.: Snow Lion, 1993.

Lati Rinbochay and Jeffrey Hopkins. *Death, Intermediate State, and Rebirth in Tibetan Buddhism*. Ithaca, N.Y.: Snow Lion, 1980.

Lhalungpa, Lobsang, trans. *The Life of Milarepa*. London: Granada, 1979.

Mackenzie, Vickie. *Reincarnation: The Boy Lama*. Boston: Wisdom, 1996.

Mullin, Glenn H. *The Practice of Kalachakra*. Ithaca, N.Y.: Snow Lion, 1991.

————, ed. *Readings on the Six Yogas of Naropa.* Ithaca, N.Y.: Snow Lion, 1997.

————, ed. *Selected Works of the Dalai Lama II: The Tantric Yogas of Sister Niguma.* Ithaca, N.Y.: Snow Lion, 1985.

Nalanda Translation Committee. *The Life of Marpa the Translator.* Boulder: Prajna, 1982.

Thurman, Robert A. F., trans. and ed. *Life and Teachings of Tsongkhapa.* Dharamsala: Library of Tibetan Works and Archives, 1982.

Tsong-ka-pa. *Tantra in Tibet: The Great Exposition of Secret Mantra.* Translated and edited by Jeffrey Hopkins. London: George Allen & Unwin, 1977.

————. *The Yoga of Tibet: The Great Exposition of Secret Mantra, Parts 2 and 3.* Translated and edited by Jeffrey Hopkins. London: George Allen & Unwin, 1977.

Yeshe, Lama Thubten. *Introduction to Tantra: A Vision of Totality.* Compiled and edited by Jonathan Landaw. Boston: Wisdom, 1987.

————. *The Tantric Path of Purification: The Yoga Method of Heruka Vajrasattva.* Compiled, edited, and annotated by Nicholas Ribush. Boston: Wisdom, 1995.

Yeshe, Lama Thubten and Thubten Zopa Rinpoche. *Wisdom Energy.* Boston: Wisdom. 1982.

Index

About the Author

Lama Thubten Yeshe (1935–84) was born in Tibet and educated at the great Sera Monastic University. He fled the Chinese oppression in 1959, and in the late 1960s, with his chief disciple Lama Thubten Zopa Rinpoche, he began teaching Buddhism to Westerners at Kopan Monastery in Kathmandu, Nepal. In 1975 they founded the international Buddhist organization the Foundation for the Preservation of the Mahayana Tradition (FPMT), which now has more than 160 centers, projects, and services worldwide.

Robina Courtin has been ordained since the late 1970s and has worked full time since then for Lama Thubten Yeshe and Lama Zopa Rinpoche's FPMT. Over the years she has served as editorial director of Wisdom Publications, editor of *Mandala* magazine, executive director of Liberation Prison Project, and as a touring teacher of Buddhism. Her life and work with prisoners have been featured in the documentary films *Chasing Buddha* and *Key to Freedom*.

To find out more about the FPMT, contact:

FPMT International Office
1632 SE 11th Avenue
Portland, OR 97214-4702 USA
Telephone: 503-808-1588 • Fax: 503-808-159
fpmt.org

Also Available by Lama Yeshe from Wisdom Publications

Becoming the Compassion Buddha
Tantric Mahamudra for Everyday Life
Edited by Robina Courtin, foreword by Geshe Lhundub Sopa

Becoming Vajrasattva
The Tantric Path of Purification
Edited by Nick Ribush
Foreword by Lama Zopa Rinpoche

Mahamudra
How to Discover Our True Nature

Introduction to Tantra
The Transformation of Desire
Edited by Jonathan Landaw, foreword by Philip Glass

When the Chocolate Runs Out
A "Little Book of Wisdom"

Wisdom Energy
Basic Buddhist Teachings
With Lama Zopa Rinpoche

About Wisdom Publications

Wisdom Publications is the leading publisher of classic and contemporary Buddhist books and practical works on mindfulness. To learn more about us or to explore our other books, please visit our website at wisdomexperience.org or contact us at the address below.

Wisdom Publications
199 Elm Street
Somerville, MA 02144 USA

We are a 501(c)(3) organization, and donations in support of our mission are tax deductible.

Wisdom Publications is affiliated with the Foundation for the Preservation of the Mahayana Tradition (FPMT).